WITH
BOTH EYES
OPEN

WITH
BOTH EYES
OPEN

Seeing
Beyond Gender

EDITED BY
PATRICIA ALTENBERND JOHNSON
AND
JANET KALVEN

THE PILGRIM PRESS
NEW YORK

Copyright © 1988 The Pilgrim Press

All rights reserved

No part of this publication may be reproduced, stored in a
retrieval system, or transmitted in any form or by any means,
electronic, mechanical, photocopying, recording, or otherwise (brief quotations used in magazine or newspaper reviews excepted), without the prior permission of the publisher.

The biblical quotations in this book are from the *Revised
Standard Version of the Bible,* copyright 1946, 1952, and
© 1971, 1973 by the Division of Christian Education, National Council of Churches, and are used by permission.

Library of Congress Cataloging-in-Publication Data

With both eyes open.
   Bibliography: p.
   Includes index.
   1. Feminism.   2. Women—History. I. Johnson, Patricia
Altenbernd, 1945–   . II. Kalven, Janet, 1913–   .
HQ1206.W76   1988   305.4'2   87-36050
          ISBN 0-8298-0777-2 (pbk.)

The Pilgrim Press, 132 West 31 Street
New York, NY 10001

HQ
1206
. W76
1988

JESUIT - KRAUSS - McCORMICK - LIBRARY
1100 EAST 55th STREET
CHICAGO, ILLINOIS 60615

FOR RITA, JANET,
LINDA, JUDY, MARCIE, LORRAINE,
AND JOANN

Contents

vii

Contributors

ELIZABETH DODSON GRAY is an environmentalist and futurist, author, lecturer, and codirector, with her husband, David Dodson Gray, of the Bolton Institute for a Sustainable Future, which she describes as "a mom and pop think tank run on a shoestring." In her essay in this volume, and in her books *Green Paradise Lost* (Wellesley 1979) and *Patriarchy as a Conceptual Trap* (Wellesley 1982), she weaves together her environmental, feminist, and religious concerns. She emphasizes the nonhierarchical view of the universe being developed through feminist theologizing and shows its consequences for male/female relationships and for the future of planet Earth.

SANDRA G. HARDING teaches at the University of Delaware, where she is Professor of Philosophy and Director of Women's Studies and has a joint appointment to the Sociology Department. She has published numerous articles and books on gender issues, including *Discovering Reality: Feminist Perspectives on Epistemology, Metaphysics, Methodology and Philosophy of Science* (co-edited with Merrill Hintikka) and *The Science Question in Feminism*. Her work analyzes the ways in which the sciences, despite their claims to objectivity, reflect unexamined race, sex, and class biases. She points the way to a new understanding of objectivity founded on an explicit commitment to emancipatory values.

ANN SUTHERLAND HARRIS, Professor of Art History at the University of Pittsburgh, was cocurator, with Linda Nochlin, of the first international exhibition of art by women, *Women Artists 1550–1950,* which toured the United States in 1976. This exhibit and the accompanying book represent a major event in the art world, presenting a broad historical survey of the contributions of women painters from the Renaissance to the mid-twentieth century through 158 works by eighty-four European and American artists. She is a founder of the National Museum of Women in the Arts, which opened in Washington, D.C., in 1986.

PATRICIA ALTENBERND JOHNSON is Associate Professor of Philosophy and Director of Women's Studies at the University of Dayton. Her areas of research include philosophy of religion, nineteenth- and twentieth-century German philosophy, and philosophical hermeneutics. She has published in many journals, including *Union Seminary Quarterly Review, Philosophy Today, Idealistic Studies,* and *Social Studies of Science.* Her work in feminist education includes helping to establish and doing public relations work for the Toronto Rape Crisis Centre, teaching Philosophy and Women, and organizing interdisciplinary courses in the Women's Studies program. She coordinated the interdisciplinary series from which this book began.

JANET KALVEN is a feminist educator and activist with a long-standing interest in questions of feminism and religion. One of the group that in 1944 established Grailville in Loveland, Ohio, as a women's educational center, she has coordinated a variety of short- and long-term residential programs at Grailville, including Semester at Grailville (1968–75) and Seminary Quarter at Grailville (1974–78). She also served as Associate Director of the Self-directed Learning Program at the University of Dayton (1972–86) and as a member of the U.D. Women's Studies Committee. She is coauthor and coeditor of *Your Daughters Shall Prophesy: Feminist Alternatives in Theological Education* and *Women's Spirit Bonding.*

ANN J. LANE is Director of Women's Studies and Professor of History at Colgate University. She does research in the history of women in America, the history of slavery, and U.S. intellectual history. Her work on Mary Ritter Beard first opened for her the vision of women's place in world history and led her into feminism and women's studies. Her books include *The Brownsville Affair: National Outrage and Black Reaction, Mary*

Ritter Beard: A Source Book, The Debate over Slavery, and *The Charlotte Perkins Gilman Reader.*

LINDA C. MAJKA is Associate Professor of Sociology and Anthropology at the University of Dayton, with a special interest in social history, gender studies, and labor history. With her husband, Theo Majka, she coauthored *Farm Workers, Agribusiness and the State* (1982). She has written on farm labor movements for *Social Problems* and for *Research in Social Movements,* volume 6. She is coeditor of and contributor to *Families and Economic Distress* (1988). For the 1987–88 academic year she accepted an appointment as visiting professor at Antioch College.

JULIA REICHERT is Assistant Professor of Motion Pictures at Wright State University. A graduate of Antioch College, she began her career as a filmmaker with the documentary *Growing Up Female,* which she made together with James Klein in 1971. The first film of its kind, it brings a clearly feminist viewpoint to bear on the subtle and not-so-subtle constraints that contemporary culture places on female children. Among her other films are *Methadone, an American Way of Dealing* (1974), *Union Maids* (1976), and *Seeing Red* (1983). The latter two films received Academy Award nominations. She is one of the founders of New Day Films, a cooperative of independent filmmakers, who, since the early 1970s, have established themselves as leading distributors of films on feminism and other social issues.

ROSEMARY RADFORD RUETHER is the Georgia Harkness Professor of Applied Theology at the Garrett Evangelical Theological Seminary of Northwestern University in Evanston, Illinois, and a member of the graduate faculty at Northwestern. The author of twenty-one books and more than 435 articles in the areas of theology and social justice, she is a leading exponent of feminist theology in the United States. She pioneered in the Christian feminist critique of patriarchy with her editing of *Religion and Sexism: Images of Woman in the Jewish and Christian Traditions* (1974). She has contributed to the recovery of the hidden history

xiii

of women and religion with *Women of Spirit: Female Leadership in the Jewish and Christian Traditions* and the three-volume work *Women and Religion in America, A Documentary History*. Most recently she has undertaken the task of developing a feminist religious vision in three books: *Sexism and God-Talk, Toward a Feminist Theology* (1983), *Womanguides: Texts for Feminist Theology* (1984), and *Women-Church: Theology and Practice of Feminist Liturgical Communities* (1986).

Preface

THE ESSAYS GATHERED in this book were first presented in a lecture series at the University of Dayton in the fall of 1986. The organizers of the series, an ad hoc interdisciplinary group of women faculty, concerned to share with a wider community some of the wealth of new scholarship by and about women, appropriated Elizabeth Dodson Gray's phrasing. What would the world look like "with both eyes open"? What differences do the new perspectives make to our self-understanding as human beings, to our relationships with one another, to our educational institutions, and to our hopes for the future?

In this book seven women, speaking from ecology, history, art history, filmmaking, sociology, philosophy of science, and theology, address these questions. As organizers of the series and editors of the material, we have been privileged to share in the interdisciplinary approach and cooperation that characterized the series. The similarities in the insights from the disparate disciplines are striking, and we have endeavored to draw together some of the parallels and their implications in our introductory and concluding chapters.

The first chapter attempts to put the new scholarship by and about women into historical perspective, tracing the stages by which women have gained entry into the various fields, noting the similarity of the obstacles they have encountered in widely differing areas, assessing the current position of Women's Studies, and describing some characteristics common to the feminist approaches.

In "Eden's Garden Revisited," Elizabeth Dodson Gray offers a Christian ecological perspective. Her approach includes a critique of the patriarchal concept of the universe as a hierarchy with a chain of being that too readily becomes a chain of domination threatening the planet. She suggests a reconceptualization of reality as an interrelated web. This concept changes our self-understanding of our place as humans in the universe and of our relations to one another as different genders, races, and ethnic groups. She makes a case for the necessity of moving toward this alternative concept if humankind is to have a sustainable future on planet Earth.

Ann Lane contributes to the development of an alternative concept of humankind by taking a closer look at human history. Why are women almost invisible in history as written? Has an unconscious male bias distorted our view of the human past? What difference does a woman-centered view make to the content of history, to our notions of achievement and greatness, and to our standards of critical inquiry? Lane concludes that in claiming their past, women are shaping new categories of historical interpretation that will change the way in which history is written and understood.

There is perhaps no field in which women have been rendered more invisible than in the visual arts. Ann Sutherland Harris explores the situation of women artists in the three major fields of portraiture, still life, and figurative painting. She does this by comparing women of the sixteenth and seventeenth centuries with their modern counterparts. Her study makes vivid the particular barriers that sexist society erects in the way of artistically talented women and clarifies the ways in which conditions have and have not improved in the course of the past three centuries.

Julia Reichert, herself a distinguished maker of documentary films, discusses the entry of women into the contemporary art of filmmaking. She looks at the conditions faced by women producers and directors in Europe and North America, describes the scope of their work, and analyzes the ways in which the feminist critique is affecting the world of film.

Women in the social sciences have developed the concept of "the sex-gender system," i.e., the set of arrangements by which a society transforms biological sexual differences into socially constructed roles and relationships. Linda Majka analyzes some of the ways in which such a sex-gender system is presupposed in current work that supports a concept of free-market capitalism and that influences government policies. In particular, she looks at the ways in which free-market authors ignore or misrepresent research inconsistent with images of a patriarchal family. Such misrepresentation of the family, of the role of women, and of the attitudes toward the poor work together to increase the number of women in poverty and to push them to lower and lower levels of subsistence.

Feminist critiques of the sciences have only recently begun to appear. Sandra Harding, as a philosopher of science, offers a searching critique of the androcentrism of the scientific enterprise of the past three centuries. Moving from the apparently innocent question "Why are there so few women in science?" she shows how the feminist analysis has moved to deeper and deeper levels, challenging the sexist biases in research and in the conceptualizing of scientific work in terms of aggressive penetration of "Nature" symbolized as female. Finally, she deals with the need to reconceptualize "objectivity" in the light of a sociology of knowledge that shows the relevance of the social identity of the researcher to the results of the research.

Rosemary Radford Ruether examines the patriarchal character of Christian theology, tracing it to its roots in the Old Testament and the classical cultures of Greece and Rome. Raising the question "Can Christianity be liberated from patriarchy?" she finds hope in the antipatriarchal elements in the tradition: the prophetic themes of the Bible that proclaim a God who seeks justice for the oppressed, the liberal and liberationist movements inspired by Christianity through the centuries, and the current movements among large numbers of Christian and Jewish women, many of them theologically trained, who are seeking an alternative to the patriarchal construction of religion.

The last chapter is an assessment of where the new scholarship is taking us. What are the promises and possibilities for curriculum, for methods of teaching, and for the structure of our educational institutions? What possibilities of transformation emerge from the feminist challenge to academia's assumptions, concepts, methods, and conclusions? Does the feminist critique of method and objectivity imply a profound restructuring of knowledge itself as well as of the ways our society produces and uses knowledge? These questions lead to the realization that feminism is not simply a set of women's issues, but a perspective on the whole of reality. Where is the new perspective leading us? The contributors to this book suggest that it is leading us to a new view of humanity's place in the universe; a new picture of the human past; a profound shift in our ways of researching, learning, and teaching; a restructuring of our social institutions; and a new religious vision.

The Modern Language Association form of documentation is used in the book, the most suitable format in which to present the authors' wide range of academic disciplines and scholarships. Parenthetical citations in the text refer to a bibliography at the conclusion of each chapter. Notes also appear at the end of chapters.

We thank all the women who contributed to this book, including the authors of the various chapters and the women at the University of Dayton who developed the series that inspired it: Rita Bowen, Janet Coryell, Linda Majka, Judy Martin, Marcie May, Lorraine Murphy, and Joann Swanson. We also thank our major funders, The Fund for Christian Humanism at the University of Dayton and The Ohio Humanities Council, a state-based agency of the National Endowment for the Humanities, which makes grants to nonprofit organizations in Ohio for public programs in the humanities. Finally, we thank Lora Durham for all her work in typing the manuscript.

Patricia Altenbernd Johnson
Janet Kalven

WITH
BOTH EYES
OPEN

CHAPTER I

With Both Eyes Open

JANET KALVEN &
PATRICIA ALTENBERND JOHNSON

The human species . . . has been driving down the highway of
life with one eye (the female) held firmly closed.
—Elizabeth Dodson Gray
(*Patriarchy as a Conceptual Trap* 129)

Separate Spheres, Separate Visions

IN THE PAST TWO DECADES the United States has witnessed an
extraordinary burst of creativity in scholarship by and about
women. To appreciate the full significance of this work, it is
important to view it in historical perspective, the perspective of
centuries of the exclusion of women from public life and from
"the higher culture." The separation of human existence into
two spheres, according to sex, has a long history that has been
explained in a variety of ways. Margaret Mead suggested, in
Male and Female, that this separation can be attributed to womb
envy:

The recurrent problem of civilization is to define the male role
satisfactorily enough . . . so that the male may . . . reach a solid
sense of irreversible achievement, of which his childhood
knowledge of the satisfactions of childbearing have given him a
glimpse. . . . In a great number of human societies men's sure-
ness of their sex role is tied up with their right, or ability, to
practice some activity that women are not allowed to practice.
Their maleness in fact has to be underwritten by preventing
women from entering some field or performing some feat. . . .

There seems no evidence that it is necessary for men to surpass women in any specific way, but rather that men do need to find reassurance in achievement, and because of this connection, cultures frequently phrase achievement as something that women do not or cannot do, rather than directly as something which men do well. (159–60)

Others suggest that women, at least in the aftermath of the American Revolution, helped to define the sphere of domesticity for themselves, viewing it as an improvement of their lot.

Nancy F. Cott, in *The Bonds of Womanhood,* argues that the delineation of a woman's sphere enabled women to begin to develop a sense of their own identity: "The canon of domesticity intensified women's gender-group identification, by assimilating diverse personalities to one work-role that was also a sex-role signifying a shared and special destiny" (100). As women claimed an area of life, they developed bonds, and common abilities and ways of seeing. Although this position cannot really be called feminist, the sisterhood and vision that developed in this sphere helped to prepare the way for the contemporary feminist movement.

Whatever the reasons for the separation of the spheres of women and men, the result was the undervaluing of women's achievements and the writing of women out of history. The sphere of activity reserved for men was considered the higher sphere, and women were systematically excluded from it. In particular, women were excluded from politics, theology, law, medicine, and the arts and sciences. Human vision in these spheres has been restricted, until very recently, to the male eye alone. As Gerda Lerner observes in *The Creation of Patriarchy,*

women have "made history," yet have been kept from knowing their history and from interpreting history, either their own or that of men. Women have been systematically excluded from the enterprise of creating symbol systems, philosophies, science and law. Women have not only been educationally deprived throughout historical time in every known society, they have been excluded from theory formation. The contradiction between women's centrality and active role in creating society and their marginality in the meaning giving process of interpretation and explanation has been a dynamic force causing women to struggle against their condition. (5)

2

We are living in a time of far-reaching change in women's consciousness. There is a growing perception of the contradictions between women's actions and their interpretation; a sense of women's collective strength; a determination to share in and, if necessary, reconstruct the process of giving meaning. A brief tracing of the entrance of women into the areas considered part of the "higher culture" will help position the essays in this volume that are representative of women's recent creative work.

Gaining Entrance, Gaining Vision

The higher spheres mentioned earlier have been opened to women only recently, reluctantly and imperfectly. In the United States it was well into the nineteenth century before the first wave of the women's movement began the tasks of entry for women into higher education and of ensuring equality before the law. In 1821 Emma Willard opened her Female Seminary in Troy, New York, the first state-endowed institution for the education of women. Determined to enlarge the curriculum with subjects hitherto reserved for men, she faithfully did her own homework, each evening reciting her lessons in botany, chemistry, astronomy, and mathematics to her friend, Professor Eaton of the Rensselaer Institute, before teaching them to her classes the next day. In 1829, when the school held the first public examination of a young woman in geometry, the event was greeted with a storm of ridicule (Buhle and Buhle 62). Despite the fact that the medical opinion of the time held that the strain of higher education on women's smaller and weaker brains would damage their childbearing capacities (Ehrenreich and English 125ff.), in 1833 Oberlin opened its doors to women, becoming the first coeducational college in the United States. In 1837 Mt. Holyoke was founded as the first women's college (Gager 567), to be followed before the end of the century by the other "seven sisters" colleges, other schools for women, and by the admission of women to the public colleges and universities. By 1870 women had been admitted to some 30 percent of U.S. colleges and by 1900, to 70 percent of the institutions of higher education. In fact, by that time there were more women enrolled in coeducational institutions than in women's colleges (Walsh and Walsh 271). However, not until the late 1960s did the prestigious Ivy League schools of the northeast begin to open to women (Yale University, in 1969). The U.S. military academies followed suit in 1976.

In the political sphere the rights of women were first publicly proclaimed at the Seneca Falls Convention of 1848. It took more than seventy years of petitions, referendums, party platform and state constitutional conventions, and state and national campaigns to secure for the female citizens of this democracy the right to vote. The suffrage amendment by no means settled all the questions of women's civil rights. There is a long-standing judicial tradition of interpreting the word person in the Fifth and Fourteenth Amendments to the Constitution as not including women. As late as 1970 a federal district court upheld the exemption of women from jury duty on the ground that wives and mothers are needed at home. The message was clear: women were indispensable at home, but dispensable in the courtroom, where justice was not considered impaired if no jury of her peers was available when a woman was on trial.

In 1975 the U.S. Supreme Court finally declared such exemptions unconstitutional, but there remain on the books many discriminatory laws based on the implicit assumption that women's roles as citizens must give way to their roles as wives and mothers (Okin 262–64). In 1923 the Equal Rights Amendment was first proposed to give an unequivocal constitutional basis for eliminating discrimination based on sex, but powerful forces in church and state are still preventing its passage. Women's advances into political office have been equally slow. In 1916 Jeanette Rankin from Montana became the first woman elected to Congress; but women have never constituted more than 4 percent of the Congress, more than 2 percent of the federal judiciary (Gager 568, 541), or more than solitary tokens in the Cabinet and, finally, in the 1980s, on the Supreme Court.

In the learned professions the story is similar. By the middle of the nineteenth century the first woman had entered this male bastion. Elizabeth Blackwell received her M.D. degree in 1848, albeit from an eclectic rather than a "regular" medical school. Antoinette Brown Blackwell was ordained to the Christian ministry in 1853, although after her marriage she resigned from her ministerial duties because she found them incompatible with her role as wife and mother. Ada Kepley was graduated from law school in 1870; and in 1879 Belva Ann Lockwood, whose portrait recently appeared on a 17-cent stamp, became the first woman admitted to practice before the U.S. Supreme Court (Gager 568).

The churches have been slow to open ordination to women. The plaint of one woman minister, "My church ordained me but is not willing to employ me," has been echoed by countless others. The mainline Protestant denominations did not begin to ordain women until the 1950s; the Episcopal Church granted priesthood to women in 1974 after a bitter and divisive struggle. The Roman Catholic Church and the Greek Orthodox Church, as well as orthodox Judaism, continue to refuse women on the grounds of "tradition" or the "divine plan." Generally, women have been approved as religious educators for the young (most often as unpaid volunteers). In the early 1970s, however, there began an astonishing influx of women into graduate theological study. Between 1972 and 1983 their numbers increased from 1,000 to about 13,500, or almost 25 percent of the total enrollment in seminaries and theological schools. In the same period there was a 400 percent increase in the number of women doctoral students. These developments have paved the way for women to be in such influential roles as theologians, seminary professors, and church executives (Fiorenza and Collins 113).

In medicine the professionalization of the field in the nineteenth century, the establishment of approved medical schools, the enacting into law of licensing requirements, and the "old boys" network controlling referrals and hospital practice all worked to marginalize women (Cott and Pleck 185ff.). The Johns Hopkins Medical School did admit women from its beginning, in the 1880s, but only because it was compelled to do so by a major donor, Mary Elizabeth Garrett, who threatened to withdraw her funds unless Johns Hopkins agreed to admit women students. Johns Hopkins set a quota, limiting women to about 10 percent of each entering class, refused to grant degrees to the first women who successfully completed the course, and severely limited internships for women graduates. In the 1920s

Harvard opened its new School of Public Health to women but did not admit them as degree candidates (Gilbert and Moore 51–56). To be eligible for the public health program, the applicant had to have completed two years of medicine. At that time, however, Harvard Medical School did not admit women. To cope with the exclusion, a number of women's medical colleges were founded in the latter part of the nineteenth century, and by 1910, 6 percent of American physicians were women. In 1976 the proportion was 8.6 percent (Mandelbaum 136–37); in 1982 it was 12.8 percent (*Statistical Abstracts* 402).

In law as in medicine the professionalization of the field severely limited the opportunities for women. Before 1750, when lawsuits were commonly brought to court by the plaintiffs themselves, women as well as men could act as attorneys, although they had no legal training. Once the law became a paid profession, women were forced out (Cott and Pleck 188). Even when they had acquired the necessary training and passed the bar examination, they could be refused the right to practice, as in the case of Mrs. Myra Bradwell in 1873. The justice of the Illinois Supreme Court, in denying Bradwell's admittance to the bar, cited the common law provision that married women had no right to make contracts, and hence could not contract for their services with prospective clients (Hamilton 175). In the mid-1970s there was a marked increase in the number of women entering law schools. The percentage of women lawyers rose from 4.9 percent in 1970 to 13.8 percent in 1980 (*Statistical Abstracts* 400).

The opening of the traditionally male spheres to women happened not only slowly, but also grudgingly and with many ingenious restrictions. A few examples illustrate the difficulties. In 1892 the University of Chicago opened as a coeducational school. By 1902, three years after the founding of Phi Beta Kappa at the university, seventy-eight women and forty-six men had been admitted to the honor society. In that same year the university voted to segregate the sexes during the first two years of college. The attempt proved costly and later was quietly abandoned (Walsh and Walsh 277). A few well-endowed schools succeeded in maintaining "separate but equal" facilities for women either through coordinate colleges (Barnard at Columbia, Radcliffe at Harvard) or through totally separate women's colleges, as at Tufts, the University of Pennsylvania, and the University of Virginia (Jencks and Riesman 300).

In 1873 Ellen Swallow Richards, who had already earned a B.A. from Vassar, became the first woman to earn a bachelor's degree from the Massachusetts Institute of Technology. Under no circumstances could she be admitted to the graduate program in chemistry; however, she was allowed a classroom in which, as an unpaid volunteer, she could teach basic chemistry to high school teachers. Frustrated in her attempts to become a research scientist, she finally settled for helping to found home economics as a new practical field "educating women for right living" (Ehrenreich and English 152f.). In 1894 Sophonisba P. Breckinridge became the first woman to pass the Kentucky bar. Unable to establish herself in a law practice, she entered the University of Chicago, where in 1901 she became the first woman to earn a Ph.D. in political science. In 1904 she earned a law degree from Chicago. Thus equipped, she was qualified to become an instructor in the new department of household administration at the university. Christopher Lasch comments on her career patterns: "She was a long time in discovering her true field of interest" (Walsh and Walsh 281).

In 1847 Maria Mitchell discovered a comet and became the first woman to be admitted to the American Academy of Arts and Sciences (AAAS). Yet, in the 1850s, the members of the Academy continued to debate whether women should be allowed to become members or to attend meetings (Kohlstedt 89). In 1987 the AAAS had 2,359 members. Their statistician could not give the exact number of women members (their computer had not yet been programmed for this datum), but said that the number was very small, about thirty (telephone conversation with AAAS office, 2/17/87). As of 1987, there were seven women among the 345 scientists who have received the Nobel prize (Rosser 402). In the 1940s Helen Taussig, a pediatric cardiologist, correctly diagnosed the cause of "blue babies," and designed the operation to correct the heart defect that prevented sufficient blood from reaching the lungs. Because she was not a surgeon (internships in surgery were not open to women when she graduated from Johns Hopkins), she had to convince a surgeon to perform the operation. When it proved outstandingly successful, he was elected to the AAAS; she was not even promoted from assistant to associate professor (Gilbert and Moore 51–56).

In the 1870s Ellen Richards was required to study separately from the male students and to work in a segregated laboratory. In the 1920s, auditing a course in bacteriology at Harvard, Helen Taussig was not allowed to speak to the male students, had to sit in the back of the room, and had to work in a segregated laboratory. In the 1960s Evelyn Fox Keller reports that as a physics student, she tried to enter the lecture room after the others; otherwise, she risked being surrounded by a ring of empty chairs, since the men did not wish to sit next to such a low-status person (Rose 87). In 1966 Mary Daly, whose doctorate in theology from Fribourg qualified her for membership in the Catholic Theological Society of America, was allowed to attend the formal meetings of the Society but was refused admission into the buffet dinner that provided opportunity for informal mingling (Daly 141).

A final example emphasizes the difficulties that women have faced in gaining entrance to academia. In 1970 Women's Equity Action League and National Organization for Women brought suit against hundreds of colleges and universities, charging sex discrimination under executive orders 11246 and 11375, which forbade discrimination by federal contractors. Millions of dollars in federal contracts were withheld while the Department of Health, Education and Welfare (HEW) investigated the charges and urged the institutions to formulate affirmative action plans. At the time Harvard had $63 million in federal contracts. It had 444 full professors, all male; no women held either full or associate professorships. At a meeting to consider the HEW directive to increase the number of women faculty, Matina Horner, the president of Radcliffe and the only woman present, reports that one of the men seriously and thoughtfully asked, "How much will we have to lower our standards to fulfill these requirements?" (Gornick).

In the 1980s the universities have been opened to women, but as the above examples illustrate, sexism and misogyny have deep roots and continue to put barriers in the way of women who aspire to serious scholarship. Sometimes there are informal restrictions to full access to training opportunities, such as a tacit quota on the number of women allowed in a school or department, or a counseling system that discourages women from entering science and technology and turns them toward education, social work, psychology, or pediatrics. Financial aid systems and selection systems for awarding prestigious postgraduate appointments, like clerkships to high court justices or assistantships to Nobel prize-winning scientists, may retain elements of bias.

Having obtained the degree, women may still find that the message is, to use Florence Howe's words, "You can study here, but you can't work here." She pointed out to the Modern Language Association that whereas 55 percent of the graduate students in English are women, only 8 percent of their teachers are. Women find that search committees, impelled by affirmative action, may go through the motions of interviewing women when they have no intention of hiring a woman. They may hire women in part-time or nontenured slots. They may unconsciously use different standards when evaluating a woman for promotion, e.g., research on women in the labor force does not count as "real economic research" or is too "limited" to be worthy of reward. A number of research projects have demonstrated that the identical piece of work is rated lower by both women and men when it has a woman's rather than a man's name attached to it. Almost a century and a half since the first woman graduated from Oberlin (1841), and although women constitute about half of college students, women are still marginal in the faculties and administration of higher education. The following table shows how women are concentrated in the two-year colleges and the lowest faculty ranks.

Having become practicing professionals, women may find that their work is often deprived of due recognition. Many women pioneers have used male pseudonyms to secure a fair appraisal of their works. Thus Mary Ann Evans was published

9

Women as a Percentage of Total Full-time
Instructional Faculty, by Institutional Type
and by Rank, 1980 Academic Year

Institutional Type	Percent Female
Total	25.9
Universities	19.6
Four-year colleges	26.8
Two-year colleges	35.2
Across Institutions, by Rank	
Professor	9.8
Associate	19.4
Assistant	33.9
Instructor	51.8
Lecturer	44.7

Source: National Center for Educational Statistics, 1980, Chart
1 and Table 7.

as George Eliot and the Brontë sisters as Currer, Ellis, and
Acton Bell. Psychiatrist Helen Flanders Dunbar, one of the
most remarkable early leaders in the religion and health movement in the United States, found it necessary to drop "Helen" in
presenting her professional writings to the public (Stokes 69–
89). By accident or design, women's work is often attributed to
a male colleague (Fanny Mendelssohn's songs to her brother
Felix, Judith Leyster's paintings to her teacher Frans Hals, Col-
ette's first novels to her husband). Sometimes, as in the case of
Helen Taussig or Rosalind Franklin, when the work is produced
by a team, most of the credit goes to the male colleagues.
Sometimes the work is evaluated as "remarkable for a woman."
Almost always women's work is rendered invisible to the next
generation; books go out of print, and actions are glossed over
or dropped out of the written record.

Despite all the difficulties that have faced women in their
entrance into the male sphere, they have gained entry. This entry
has been accompanied by an outburst of intellectual and artistic
creativity that is truly remarkable. Women have begun to contribute not just to one sphere, but to a fully human vision.

The Contemporary Opening of the Female Eye

In 1964 Betty Friedan's *Feminine Mystique* hit the best-seller lists. In 1966 Friedan founded NOW. In 1968 younger women, disillusioned by their experience with male domination in the student movement and in the civil rights and peace movements, formed a loose association and erupted into public view with a demonstration against the Miss America Beauty Pageant in Atlantic City. They crowned a sheep, but contrary to press reports only too eager to find an occasion for ridicule, they did not burn any bras. Rather, they threw into trash cans various items (stiletto heels, makeup kits, hair curlers, bras, and girdles) that symbolized women's role as sex objects. For a brief and heady moment there was an outburst of guerrilla theater in the streets. WITCH (Women's International Terrorist Conspiracy from Hell) marched on Wall Street and the stock market fell (Hole and Levine 123ff.). Another group staged a sit-in in the offices of the male publisher of the venerable *The Ladies' Home Journal* and won the opportunity to edit one issue of the magazine (Hole and Levine 255). All over the country consciousness-raising groups sprang up, and women's caucuses appeared in such unlikely places as the National Council of Churches, the American Baptist Convention, the Modern Language Association, and the American Academy of Religion. Professional organizations formed committees on the status of women, and some women chose to form their own independent organizations. In the early 1970s the Association of Women in Science, the Association for Women in Mathematics, and the Caucus for Women in Statistics formed independently of their parent organizations. In all these cases the aims of the new groups were similar: the improvement of women's status in the field, greater access for women to decision-making positions in the professional associations themselves and on the editorial boards of their publications, and the facilitation of new research on women (Briscoe 157–58). At the same time hundreds of women's centers were springing up around the country for reentry women, for continuing education, for battered women, for victims of rape and sexual harassment, and for women's health. Moreover, a wide variety of women's conferences, literary events, art and music festivals, and theater performances occurred.

Nowhere was the development of the women's movement more rapid than in its intellectual arm, Women's Studies. The first women's liberation courses were offered in the free universities that sprang up on campuses in the late 1960s (Boxer 662–63). In the spring of 1969 Cornell University offered the first "official" Women's Studies course for academic credit on the topic "the female personality from a behavioral science perspective." By the fall of 1970 San Diego State was offering a complete Women's Studies program (Hole and Levine 322–29). In 1970 KNOW, a women's press in Pittsburgh, published *Female Studies I,* containing the course syllabi and bibliographies for seventeen Women's Studies courses. By 1971 there were 610 courses, and fifteen programs, five of which offered degrees, including one offering an M.A. (Howe 79). Courses and programs have gone on multiplying with undiminished vigor so that it is difficult to keep statistics up to date. In 1983 there were 452 programs, many on such elite campuses as Yale, Harvard, and MIT. The number of courses is beyond counting, but Florence Howe estimated that in 1983, there were probably more than 30,000 courses (Howe x). In 1977 the National Women's Studies Association was formed, and in 1979 it held its first annual conference at the University of Kansas, presenting 246 panels, roundtables, readings, and performances over a four-day period. In 1986 its membership directory listed almost 3,000 individual members and 307 groups, 8 of which are from other countries.

Along with the programs and courses, research centers have blossomed. In 1983 there were forty such centers. A number of scholarly journals and reviews have appeared, among them *Signs, Journal of Women in Culture and Society,* published by the University of Chicago Press; *Feminist Studies,* out of the University of Maryland; *Frontiers, A Journal of Women's Studies,* from the Women's Studies program at the University of Colorado; *Women's Studies Quarterly,* from City College of New York; *Feminist Issues,* from Rutgers; *Women's Studies International Forum; International Journal of Women's Studies,* from Canada; and *ISIS, Women's International Journal,* from Italy. A number of journals have defined for themselves a more specialized scope, among them *The Feminist Teacher; Hypatia; Journal of Feminist Studies in Religion; Sage, a Scholarly Journal on Black Women; Women and Environments; Women and Health; Women and Therapy;* and *Women Studies in Communication.*

At the conservative estimate of 30,000 courses and 10 participants to a course, there would be at least 300,000 participants, students and teachers, working in Women's Studies in any given year, engaged in raising new questions and pursuing promising lines of research and reflection. It is not surprising then that new scholarship by and about women is pouring from the presses in an ever-increasing flood. The *Women's Review of Books,* a monthly publication from the Wellesley Center for Research on Women, routinely lists in every issue more than fifty new titles in nonfiction, fiction, drama, and poetry, which represent only a partial selection from the hundreds of volumes that appear every month. Every mail brings new catalogs from the university presses and other publishers announcing yet another series on some aspect of Women's Studies. The subject category "women" used to occupy a few drawers in the card catalog of the university library; now it threatens to expand to the size of the rest of the catalog. *Women's Studies Abstracts* attempts to keep up with the flood through an annotated bibliography issued quarterly.

The Breadth of the Emerging Vision

A complete study of this mass of material is not possible here, but it is possible to trace the sequence in which the feminist wave of critical appraisal has swept through the disciplines. The first introductory courses were broadly interdisciplinary and team-taught. These were quickly followed by courses in literature and history. Deborah S. Rosenfelt, in *Female Studies X: Learning to Speak, Student Work,* notes that the largest response to her call for publishable student work came from courses in literature, language, and writing. This is hardly surprising. English is generally regarded as "a woman's field." A little knowledge of poetry and fiction was considered a suitable female accomplishment in the woman's sphere; and a little music, painting, and drawing were part of the old "finishing school" curriculum. Moreover, when women aspire to become writers, they need no elaborate or expensive equipment; pencil and paper suffice. After all, Jane Austen wrote masterpieces without even a room of her own.

The women's movement emphasized that the personal is political. This translates, in Women's Studies, into a determination to unite thought and feeling and action, which in turn requires an interdisciplinary focus. Literature courses have consciously aimed at linking literature and life. They readily moved from surveying images of women in the traditional curriculum to the work of well-known women writers, and then to the recovery of work by little-known women writers and to questions of literary criticism. Moreover, in testing the validity of the stereotypic images against women's experiences, students were led into autobiography, social commentary, and recovery of women's hidden history. Using the techniques of journal writing and small-group discussions, such literature courses also became powerful consciousness-raising experiences. Students found the courage to risk self-expression. From the beginning those working in women's studies have been eager to share their experiences and discoveries with others in the field. Quickly women, even in undergraduate courses, moved into writing for interested audiences rather than for academic grades. This approach has resulted in autobiographies, bibliographies, biographies, stories, poems, essays, and research papers. The student work collected in *Female Studies X* is among the first of many such anthologies.

Clearly work in literature overlaps with new questions in history. One question was raised repeatedly: Why are there no great women writers or artists or philosophers or reformers? An immediate response has been an immense work of compensatory history that documents the lives and accomplishments of women such as Ann Hutchinson, Susan B. Anthony, Lucretia Mott, Harriet Taylor, Sojourner Truth, and Harriet Tubman. The works of such forgotten writers as Christine de Pisan, Mary Wollstonecraft, Charlotte Perkins Gilman, Kate Chopin, Agnes Smedley, Zora Neale Hurston, and Rebecca Harding

Davis have been republished. At the same time there has been a concern to raise new questions, to explore areas previously regarded either as unchanging or as unimportant, such as family patterns, approaches to childbirth and child-raising, birth control, rape, and social reforms.

New questions in history quickly led to new explorations in the social sciences: the studies of sex roles and the division of labor, cross-cultural comparisons of kinship structures and processes of socialization, and candid appraisals of power differentials between men and women and what might be done about them. Rayna Reiter introduces her book *Toward an Anthropology of Women* with a forthright statement:

> This book has its roots in the women's movement. To explain and describe equality and inequality between the sexes contemporary feminism has turned to anthropology with many questions in its search for a theory and a body of information. These questions are more than academic. The answers will help feminists in the struggle against sexism in our own society. (11)

She adds a warning that male bias makes anthropological discourse suspect. "All our information must be filtered through a critical lens to examine the biases inherent in it," (11) a task that her book attempts to undertake.

Inspired by a similar critical perspective, practitioners in Women's Studies called into play psychology, economics, and political science. One notable early work is Jo Freeman's *The Politics of Women's Liberation,* a brilliant study of the origins and growth of a social movement by someone who had experienced it from the inside and was able to unite personal observations and feelings with carefully assembled data and keen analysis.

At the same time there was a great outpouring of women's creativity in all the arts. In poetry and fiction the work of black women writers, such as Alice Walker, Toni Morrison, Paula Marshall, Maya Angelou, Audre Lorde, and Nikki Giovanni, has been especially significant. Women have entered music not simply as performers, but also as composers, creators of combos and bands, and producers of audio and video materials. Thousands flock to the annual women's music festivals in various parts of the country. There has been a rediscovery of some of the great black women composers of the jazz era, such as

Mary Lou Williams and Alberta Hunter, whose work has been obscured by the fame of their male contemporaries and co-workers. In the forms that require more funding and more support from society at large, women's work reveals a special level of struggle. Antonia Brico has endeavored to develop a career as a conductor of a major symphony orchestra but has been frustrated. Women film producers and directors face difficulties discussed in Julia Reichert's essay, and the creative work of women's theater groups seldom reaches even off-off Broadway.

The wave of feminist critique has been slowest to touch the natural sciences. In part this has to do with the relatively small number of women in the field. In 1974 whereas one in three Ph.D.s in psychology went to women, the proportion was only one in ten in chemistry and mathematics, and one in twenty-four in physics (Vetter 713–14). Women scientists are still rarities, underrepresented, underpromoted, and underpaid. They are concentrated at the lower levels of professional work as laboratory assistants and as instructors in beginning courses. They are more likely than their male counterparts to get discouraged and leave science altogether. In 1977 a study of women and minorities by the National Science Foundation reported that 47 percent of all women scientists and engineers left the labor force (Aldrich 128). Natural science is so clearly defined as a male activity that it is difficult to be both a feminist and a scientist. As Sandra Harding points out in chapter 7, conceptualizing scientific method in terms of an aggressive and penetrating assault on "Nature" symbolized as female is hardly attractive to women. The approach of Women's Studies, beginning as it does with affirming the experience of the individual woman, lends itself much more readily to work in the humanities and the social sciences.

Most often the connection between Women's Studies and the natural sciences has been on the issues of women's health, sexuality, and reproductive powers. In the 1980s three factors have highlighted the importance of a feminist critique of science: the development of genetic engineering, in vitro fertilization, and surrogate motherhood with its impact on women's lives; the rapidity of technological change in the workplace and its implications for the division of labor; and the revival of biological determinism in sociobiology. All three factors have combined to produce a relatively recent and rapid increase in feminist critiques of science. A bibliography published in *Feminist Approaches to Science* lists eighty-four references, none from the 1960s and 78 percent from the period 1980–84 (Bleier).

The Depth of the Emerging Vision

Although work in Women's Studies has rapidly swept through the disciplines, it has also begun to establish itself in particular disciplines in a more pervasive and transformative manner. History serves as a good exemplification of the depth of the emerging vision.

First, there was an awareness of the absence of women from history as written. College classes asked to list the names of women, other than entertainers and athletes or presidents' wives, who have done significant work and helped to make history, can seldom come up with even five names. We see what we are trained to see, and we are trained to see political figures, generals, and great male artists and thinkers as historically significant. The awareness that women are missing leads to an initial critique that primarily consists of totaling the percentages of women listed in history books, the general histories, and the histories of special fields, such as art, science, and religion. As Gerda Lerner points out in *The Creation of Patriarchy,* women constitute half the human race and have been active at all times and places, helping to build society and keep it going. Women are not absent from history; they have been rendered invisible in the written record.

This insight leads to compensatory history. Archives are searched for records of women's activities; out-of-print books are republished; new biographies are written. However, for the most part, the hidden history that is thus recovered is fitted into the established categories: the queens and abbesses of medieval and early modern times; the royal mistresses who wielded power behind the throne; and particular individuals of importance, such as George Eliot, George Sand, Marie Curie, Mar-

17

garet Fuller, Louisa May Alcott, Clara Barton, Dorothea Dix, and Jane Addams. The recipe is "add women and stir." The historian's attention has been directed to a few gaps in the record. These outstanding women emerge, like isolated mountain peaks. They are accommodated by adding a paragraph here, a bibliographic reference there. The historian is still looking with a single, patriarchal eye.

But the nagging questions persist. Why are there so few outstanding women? Why are women's roles and activities valued so little? Some scholars turn to the lives of ordinary women. They reconstruct some patterns by asking new questions of such standard resources as the demographic data. How long did the average woman live? At what age did she usually marry? At what age did she have her first child? How many children did she have? What were the rates of maternal and infant mortality? What percentage remained single? What percentage were widowed? What records are there of women's economic activity in the home and outside it?

The search for documentation widens beyond the conventional sources because these have not preserved this information. The search leads to collections of family papers, to women's letters and diaries moldering in attics or basements or in uncataloged collections in local historical societies. It embraces oral histories, records of such nonpolitical women's groups as social and literary clubs, church societies, sewing circles, women's magazines, and popular fiction. It turns also to artifacts, such as quilts, pottery, weaving, and embroidery, that have been produced by women.

The focus shifts from what men have written about women to women's own descriptions of their experiences. Once the female eye has opened, whole new areas emerge as requiring study: domestic work and domestic workers, sexuality, changing attitudes toward sexual pleasure, social movements initiated or carried forward by women, women's health and women's dress, midwifery and its demise at the hands of the medical profession. History becomes the process of women claiming their past and building a new consciousness of their foremothers' lives, work, options, sufferings, and achievements.

As the categories emerge from the materials, and as women

historians approach the materials with a feminist consciousness, a profound process of reconceptualization begins. More questions emerge as significant. Is periodization the same for both men and women? Were the great periods of Western civilization, such as Periclean Athens and the Renaissance, great for women, or did they represent a narrowing of women's options? Because women have been excluded from political and military power, we might expect that periodization based on these categories would bear little relation to women's lives. Perhaps the crucial turning points in women's history are best identified by looking at the effects on women's lives of major shifts in the modes of production, changes in the quality and availability of health care, or the advent of fairly reliable contraception. Do such changes have the same impact on the lives of women of different classes? Were the greater opportunities available to middle-class women in the nineteenth century dependent in part on the availability of low-wage black and immigrant domestic workers? Is the very notion of "class" applicable to women in the same sense as to men? A woman's class is determined by the status of her husband or father, but a middle-class woman has very different access to leisure, power, money, or occupations than the males of her class. By what standards do we evaluate human achievement? Why do societies honor the sex that kills and not the sex that gives birth?

It has taken 150 years for women to break the barriers and enter in significant numbers into higher education, the learned professions, and serious scholarship. In the 1980s women are a majority of the students in higher education, and almost all U.S. colleges and universities have become coeducational. However, as Florence Howe demonstrates, coeducation "has meant the admission of women into male-initiated, male centered, and male controlled institutions" (Howe 209). The nineteenth-century reformers fought for women's right to study the same curriculum as their brothers. Women had first to prove themselves, to show that they could master the disciplines and their methods. It is not until the past two decades, with the new awarenesses stimulated by the women's movement, that feminist critiques of the male curriculum have emerged, pointing out that the traditional curriculum could aptly be called Men's Studies, since it consists almost entirely of works written by men about men, their achievements, and their concerns.

Every critique implies an alternative, and women in every field have begun to make the alternatives explicit. Something new is happening. Women have moved from seeing themselves as competent scholars to seeing themselves as creators of new knowledge, shapers of culture. In 1964 David Riesman could write in the introduction to *Academic Women* by Jessie Bernard,

> women prefer to be teachers, passing on a received heritage and responsively concerning themselves with their students, while men of equivalent or even lesser abilities prefer to be men-of-knowledge, breaking the accustomed mold. (xvii)

In the past two decades feminist scholars have become women-of-knowledge, breaking the accustomed mold, trusting their own experience and insights, asking new questions, opening up new fields of inquiry, challenging established disciplines and proposing profound restructurings "of knowledge, the university and society" (Boxer 677).

The work of researching and writing women's history has begun, but no one knows how many generations of scholars will be needed to produce a women's history that can enter into true dialogue with traditional patriarchal history. True dialogue is between peers. Only out of such dialogue can the task of writing human history as a picture of the past in its full human reality be accomplished.

The Essays in This Book

The essays in this book all represent this deepening feminist critique. Each author addresses her own field, asking questions and using approaches that emerge out of women's experiences. Although the fields are diverse, there are commonalities in the vision and in the recognition of the need for transformation. The preamble of the Constitution of the National Women's Studies Association states:

> Women's Studies, diverse as its components are, has at its best shared a vision of a world free not only from sexism but also

from racism, class-bias, ageism, heterosexual bias—from all the ideologies and institutions that have consciously or unconsciously oppressed and exploited some for the advantage of others. . . . The uniqueness of women's studies has been its refusal to accept sterile divisions between academy and community, between the growth of the mind and the health of the body, between intellect and passion, between the individual and society. Women's studies then is equipping women not only to enter society as whole and productive human beings, but to transform it. (4)

All the essays in this book contribute to this goal.

Moreover, by addressing important questions and offering difficult challenges, these essays contribute to a transformation that facilitates not only the freedom and vision of women, but also the freedom and vision of all humanity. This work helps all humans to begin to see and understand "with both eyes open."

Works Cited

Aldrich, Michele. "Women in Science." *Signs* 4 (1978):126–35.

Bernard, Jessie. *Academic Women.* University Park, PA: Pennsylvania State University Press, 1964.

Bleier, Ruth, ed. *Feminist Approaches to Science.* Elmsford, NY: Pergamon Press, 1986.

Boxer, Marilyn. "For and About Women: The Theory and Practice of Women's Studies in the United States." *Signs* 7 (1982):661–95.

Briscoe, Anne M. "Phenomenon of the Seventies: The Women's Caucuses." *Signs* 4 (1978):152–58.

Buhle, Mary Jo, and Paul Buhle, eds. *The Concise History of Woman Suffrage.* Chicago: University of Illinois Press, 1978.

Carroll, Bernice A., ed. *Liberating Women's History.* Chicago: University of Illinois Press, 1976.

Cott, Nancy F. *The Bonds of Womanhood.* New Haven, CT: Yale University Press, 1977.

———, and Elizabeth H. Pleck. *A Heritage of Her Own, Toward a New Social History of American Women.* New York: Simon & Schuster, 1979.

Daly, Mary. *The Church and the Second Sex.* New York: Harper & Row, 1975.

Ehrenreich, Barbara, and Deirdre English. *For Her Own Good,* 150

Years of the Experts' Advice to Women. Garden City, NY: Doubleday, 1979.

Fiorenza, Elisabeth Schüssler, and Mary Collins. *Women Invisible in Church and Theology,* Concilium 182. Edinburgh: T. & T. Clark, 1985.

Freeman, Jo. *The Politics of Women's Liberation: A Case Study of an Emerging Social Movement and Its Relation to the Policy Process.* New York: David McKay, 1975.

Friedan, Betty. *The Feminine Mystique.* New York: Dell, 1963.

Gager, Nancy, ed. *Women's Rights Almanac.* New York: Harper & Row, 1975.

Gilbert, Lynn, and Gaylen Moore. *Particular Passions, Talks with Women Who Have Shaped Our Times.* New York: Crown, 1981.

Gornick, Vivian. "Why Radcliffe Women Are Afraid of Success." *N.Y. Times Magazine,* 14 January 1973, 61.

Gray, Elizabeth Dodson. *Patriarchy as a Conceptual Trap.* Wellesley, MA: Roundtable Press, 1982.

Hamilton, Mary Jane. "A History of Married Women's Rights." In *Women and Men,* edited by Dana V. Hiller and Robin Ann Sheets. Cincinnati: Office of Women's Studies, University of Cincinnati, 1977.

Hiller, Dana V., and Robin Ann Sheets, eds. *Women and Men, The Consequences of Power.* Cincinnati: Office of Women's Studies, University of Cincinnati, 1977.

Hole, Judith, and Ellen Levine. *Rebirth of Feminism.* New York: Quadrangle Books, 1971.

Howe, Florence. *Myths of Coeducation.* Bloomington: Indiana University Press, 1984.

Jencks, Christopher, and David Riesman. *The Academic Revolution.* Garden City, NY: Doubleday, 1968.

Kohlstedt, Sally Gregory. "In from the Periphery: American Women in Science, 1830–1880." *Signs* 4 (1978):81–96.

Lerner, Gerda. *The Creation of Patriarchy.* New York: Oxford University Press, 1986.

Mandelbaum, Dorothy Rosenthal. "Women in Medicine." *Signs* 4 (1978):136–37.

Mead, Margaret. *Male and Female.* New York: Wm. Morrow, 1949.

National Women's Studies Association Constitution. *1st NWSA Conference Program.* College Park: University of Maryland, 1979.

Okin, Susan Moller. *Women in Western Political Thought.* Princeton, NJ: Princeton University Press, 1979.

Reiter, Rayna, ed. *Toward an Anthropology of Women.* New York: Monthly Review Press, 1975.

Rose, Hilary. "Hand, Brain, and Heart: A Feminist Epistemology for the Natural Sciences." *Signs* 9 (1983):73–90.

Rosenfelt, Deborah Silverton. *Female Studies X: Learning to Speak, Student Work.* Old Westbury, NY: The Feminist Press, 1975.

Rosser, Sue V. Reviews of *Women in Science: A Report from the Field,* edited by Jane Butler Kahle, and *Myths of Gender: Biological Theories About Women and Men,* edited by Anne Fausto-Sterling. *Signs* 12 (1987):402–5.

Scott, Ann Firor, ed. *The American Woman: Who Was She?* Englewood Cliffs, NJ: Prentice-Hall, 1971.

Statistical Abstracts of the U.S., 1986.

Stokes, Allison. *Ministry After Freud.* New York: The Pilgrim Press, 1985.

Vetter, Betty M. "Women in the Natural Sciences." *Signs* 1 (1975):713–14.

Walsh, Mary R., and Francis Walsh. "The Crisis in Coeducation." In *Women and Men,* edited by Dana V. Hiller and Robin Ann Sheets. Cincinnati: Office of Women's Studies, University of Cincinnati, 1977.

CHAPTER 2

Eden's Garden Revisited
A Christian Ecological Perspective

ELIZABETH DODSON GRAY

What We See

FOR THOSE OF US with sight, we open our eyes each morning and receive the visual message of a new day. Our eyes are our two windows on visual reality.

But contemporary research scientists have learned that we are not able to absorb the thousands of bits of data that come in to us each moment through our eyes and ears, through our sense of touch, and through our smell and taste. Therefore, we have to filter and select. We let some bits of data register on our consciousness and some we just do not ever let through the filter.

Our filters are constructed from the way in which we view our world. We live in our minds within what those who study the sociology of knowledge have called "a social construction of reality." Humans together literally *construct* the reality, the culture, the view of the world around us. That social construction then guides what we notice and what we do not notice. Even when we notice things we perceive them through the mental filter of the intellectual categories that we have inherited along with our culture's social construction of reality. For example, we see a yellow blur and the word *daffodil* or *jonquil* swims into our mind, and we perceive that yellow blur as *flower, plant, daffodil*. We see a green blur and perceive that as *tree*, and our understanding of trees literally affects what we expect to see, and hence how we *see* that tree.

24

What I am talking about is developed at length by Peter Berger and Thomas Luckmann in *The Social Construction of Reality*, whose work in turn builds on Karl Mannheim's. All of them explore the relationship between thought and the social context in which that thought arises. For example, it must be clear to all of us that blacks did not dream up the mythology of black and white in which we live, in which things are either "black" or "white." White is associated with cleanliness, with godliness, with purity; and black is associated with dirt, with ugliness, with darkness, with sin. No black person would dream up such a mythology based on those colors; the people who dreamed that up were white!

So there is an interesting relationship between *who* is doing the thinking and *what* it is we think, and *how* indeed we do that thinking. When we first hear this we tend to draw back from it and say, "Oh, come now. Isn't a fact really a fact?" But consider this incident from our American history.

When the Spanish-American War was declared, the U.S. Navy sent an American gunboat into the harbor at Guam, and it fired on the Spanish fort in the harbor. The Spanish commander, however, had not received news that Spain and the United States were at war, so he had himself rowed out to the American gunboat to apologize in person for the fact that he could not return their ceremonial salute because *he* was out of gunpowder! This incident from our past is such a wonderful example because it shows that even if you are fired on, you don't *think* that you are being fired on *unless you have reason to believe* that you are being fired on!

Think also about paper money. The intrinsic value of each piece of paper money is clearly only the worth of the paper it is printed on. But we all agree as a culture that one piece of paper is worth only a dollar, another is worth a hundred dollars, and still another is worth a thousand dollars. As long as everyone agrees, we are in good shape and it all works.

My husband and I work at home and we have a cat. From time to time we wonder what our cat makes of what we do with our lives because we spend our lives seemingly obsessed with paper. We get up in the morning and we read the paper. We write on paper; we type on paper. Then we fold up this paper and put it in other paper. We spend our days dealing with the paper that comes into our house and that we send out. Our cat must think this is absurd—big people who could do whatever they want and they spend their lives obsessed with paper! When our cat wants to communicate with us how dumb she thinks this is, she comes and sits on the paper and, in effect, she says, "Now, what's really important is that it is time for you to stroke me and forget all that paper."

All this is clearly about reality "read in." *We* decide that all this paper and the symbols we place on it really are important to us and have this tremendous value. We do this in other ways too, for example, in how we value ourselves as human beings compared with a wooden chair that a human might own and sit on. *We* are humans; we are alive. A wooden chair is inanimate, mere wood, way down on our scale of value. We humans are important people, we think. We talk with one another; we communicate with God and go to the moon and do all kinds of wonderful things.

But since the 1920s experts in subatomic physics have known that at the subatomic level, a wooden chair and you and I are all the same *probability patterns of energy.* What they have been saying is that at the *heart of everything,* we are exactly the same invisible patterns of energy, actually *probability* patterns of energy. Therefore, the great difference we "read in" between us and a wooden chair is a mental construct of our own doing, which, at the subatomic level, simply does not hold up.

The Effects of Where You Stand on What You See

Subatomic physics has taught us some other lessons as well. For example, the observer cannot be separated from the observed. It went like this: Scientists in the 1910s and 1920s were studying the nature of light, and they discovered, using one technology, that light, at the subatomic level, is a probability pattern, a wave. However, if they viewed light in another way, using a different technology, that same light consisted, at the subatomic level, of particles. And they discovered that both test results, although contradictory, are also true; it just depends on which standing point you chose. Scientists who write about this said that it really boggled their minds because they come from a cultural tradition that says that light cannot be both wave and particle—that one or the other can be true but not both, for they are different, mutually exclusive. Scientists have written that they had to adopt almost a Zen-like mind-set in order to wrap their minds around their discovery that light is two different things and yet is both.

Several years ago a philosopher translated this into the statement "Reason is standpoint dependent." This means that every time you reason, your reasoning manifests your standing point in very subtle but very pervasive ways. For example, recall what you read in school about Columbus *discovering* America. Does that mean that America was *lost* until Columbus and Western civilization discovered it? It took hundreds of years for the Native Americans finally to answer Columbus. Several years ago when the World Council of Churches General Assembly was held in Vancouver, a Native American chief got up and, among his other remarks, said, "As far as the Native Americans are concerned, Columbus and his men were a few white men lost at sea." And indeed they were lost. They thought they were some place (India) where they were not. So, you see, even lostness and foundness are very standpoint dependent.

What all this adds up to is that there is no such thing as "objective" knowledge, not in science, not in history, not any place. There is nothing that humans think that is not influenced by their standing point: by race, class, and culture; and by sex and gender. That sex and gender constitute a standing point has escaped our notice until recently. When I was a history major at Smith College, some thirty-five years ago, I remember that we were required as history majors to take a last course, something called 40b. I now know that it was teaching a sophisticated sociology of knowledge. But I did not appreciate that at the time. The purpose of 40b was to convince us, as history majors, that there is no such thing as "objective" knowledge. Until 40b we had known that any interpretation of the historical facts was exactly that, an interpretation. The purpose of 40b was to take us far enough into the facts to realize that any fact was itself also an interpretation.

Let me tell you how this goes. If I had to write one sentence about this moment in time that you and I are sharing, what would I write: who here is white and who is black; who is male and who is female; the temperature of your room; what I am saying; or what you are wearing? What one fact would I choose about this moment in time? You can see that my filtering out a million things and selecting one thing is itself an incredible interpretation—and that choice of mine then parades as a fact. But it is really no more a fact than all the other million things I did *not* select.

This is what Women's Studies has started saying about history. Women have said it is literally "his-story" in which males looked at what humans were doing and chose to notice only what *men* were doing in most historical epochs—the battles that men were fighting, the kings who were reigning, those kinds of things. And what women were doing, what minorities were doing, what the poor were doing was considered to be of little or no historical consequence. It was not worth writing down or thinking about. And that judgment itself was an important interpretation.

Recently the whole discussion of white racism has attempted to sensitize whites to the ways in which we, as whites, construct a social construction of reality from a *white* point of view. We live in a culture that is not only a social construction of reality, but also one constructed from a number of points of view. Feminists have made us aware that we live within what they have labeled "patriarchy," a social construction of reality done from the *male* point of view. My husband has drawn a cartoon about this that shows a male figure standing within a bubble labeled "Adam's Place." The caption paraphrases Adam just as Genesis says: "I have named everything, thought everything, from *my* point of view." Adam's bubble in the cartoon is his social construction of reality. But what is interesting is that when you grow up *within* a social construction of reality and you accept it as "the truth," you then believe that this really *is* the way the world is and that this is the *only* way to look at anything.

We are just beginning to notice that all of us are living in

28

Adam's world, a world named and intellectually constructed from the male point of view. Talking about "Adam's world" is my shorthand response to people who want to know what really *is* women's problem. Women's problem, my friends, is trying to live as a woman in Adam's world. It is like wearing a suit of clothes that does not quite fit you. It roughly fits, in the sense that we are all human, that we have feelings, we have minds, we have two legs and two arms and one head. But a lot of the instinctive patterns of thinking and the way the world is looked at can be traced to the male life-experience. In subtle ways these experiences do not match women's experience, and we are just beginning to uncover the full extent of those mismatches.

Taking a Second Look in Adam's World

My husband and I had been sharing in the Episcopalian ministry for fifteen years when we came out of our parish-centered ministry and life. I was rather fresh out of the female world of rearing my children. I had spent a lot of time with other women, and I had lived my life in my home as well as with my husband in our ministry. Suddenly I was in an interesting and intellectually rich environment at the Massachusetts Institute of Technology Sloan School of Management, which, in the early 1970s, was just becoming inundated with computers and computer technology. I was told that when computers work they are "up," and when computers do not work they are "down."

I found myself thinking that was rather bizarre because when my washing machine at home did not work it was just "broken." Somehow I kept asking myself about where all this up/down computer jargon came from. One day the relationship between the male genital anatomy and "up" and "down" finally came to me. It is a natural metaphor that rises naturally out of the male life-experience. It does *not* rise naturally out of my woman's life-experience. I have also found it interesting these past few years to find male colleagues at Harvard Divinity School realizing that they no longer want to use expressions such as "the *thrust* of his thinking" or "what a *penetrating* argument" or "that was *seminal* thinking." They have realized that these ways of speaking are like the psychologist's Rorschach test, an unaware projection into their scholarly vocabulary of the male life-experience.

The role of language is important in sustaining any social construction of reality. Those today who quibble with women's concerns about inclusive language do not have a sociologically trained understanding of what happens in a social construction of reality. Berger and Luckmann devote several chapters of *The Social Construction of Reality* to language because they are totally clear that language is one of the main pillars that supports a social construction of reality. Let me give one small example that I use in my book *Patriarchy as a Conceptual Trap*. The Eskimos have about forty words that they use to describe and think about snow. We have a few: snow, slush, powder, ice. This allows us to think only minimally about snow while the richer Eskimo distinctions allow them to think with great nuances about snow conditions. Every time you say the congressman-he, the legislator-he, the president-he, chairman-of-the-board-he, you are slowly and systematically convincing every male child listening that it is right that men will occupy those jobs. And you convince every female child listening that it is somehow not right that women occupy those jobs.

Let me tell you how thorough this is. I have friends who had very unorthodox roles as mother and father and were raising young children. Their daughter had always gone to a female pediatrician, and when at age five she was asked what she wanted to be when she grew up, she said, "I want to be a nurse." The person then asked, "Why wouldn't you want to be a doctor?" The daughter replied, "Only men can be doctors. Only boys can be doctors, not girls." At this point her mother said, "But don't you realize that Dr. So-and-So, who you have been going to since you were a baby, is a *woman* doctor?" This little girl, deeply socialized in our culture, said, "She can't be; girls are nurses and men are doctors." Even her own real-life experience with a woman pediatrician had not convinced her to the contrary. So language is incredibly important.

Conceptual Errors

Living in Adam's world as we do involves for all of us two large conceptual errors. The first conceptual error is the illusion that the human is the male and the male is the human. This illusion assumes that when you get the thinking of men about theology, philosophy, psychology, science, math, anything, then you have discovered all that *humans* can think about all these things. We have lived this way for many long years. It did not occur to me when I graduated from Yale Divinity School in 1954 that all the theology I had studied there had been done by males (Saint Paul, Saint Augustine, Saint Thomas, Luther, Calvin, and so on). It simply never occurred to me that all the philosophy I had studied in college was all done by males (Aristotle, Kant, Whitehead, and so on). It never occurred to me then that all the psychology of the human had been done by males (Freud, Jung, Skinner, and so on).

Perhaps you are familiar with Lawrence Kohlberg's work at Harvard in which he set out to discover how humans do moral reasoning—and the only people he asked were adolescent males. What Kohlberg found were six stages of progressively more refined and abstract moral reasoning. He then discovered that women never got past stage three in this hierarchy of stages. When his teaching colleague Carol Gilligan set out to do her work, she decided to check out Kohlberg's work, which had been based on responses to hypothetical moral situations. What, Gilligan asked, is the moral thinking of people facing real-life moral choices? Her initial focus was moral reasoning of young men about whether to be conscientious objectors or to go into the U.S. Army and fight in the Vietnam war. The war ended and with it ended these real-life moral choices, so Gilligan chose to study the abortion choice.

Quite by accident Gilligan acquired an all-female data base. What she discovered was that women do moral reasoning very differently. They do it in a very relational way, in a "I must not hurt anybody" way. They come out with what Gilligan calls "an ethic of responsibility," as contrasted to Kohlberg and his all-male data base, which came out with "an ethic of rights." One

31

thing that confuses the pro-choice/pro-life struggles about abortion is that the pro-choice people have to function within an arena of moral discourse preoccupied about rights, even though that is not the way women do moral thinking about having or not having an abortion (or anything else). In many ways we are stuck with this "ethic of rights" as the only recognized way of thinking in our culture.

This, then, is the first conceptual error, the view that the human is normatively male, and if you see how men do it, you've seen all you need to see.

Now within Adam's world what has happened to women? How much work, paid and unpaid, do you think women do? How much income do they get? And how much ownership of property and wealth are women's worldwide? Women worldwide are one third of the paid labor force, but they, in addition, do four fifths of the informal or unpaid work of the world. That means feeding and taking care of children, taking care of the house, removing the dirt, and so on, whenever that is *not* done for pay. For all that women do, both paid and unpaid, women get only 10 percent of the world's income. And women own 1 percent of the world's wealth or property.[1] *That* is what being female in Adam's world means for women worldwide!

With One Eye Closed

The confusion of the male with the human is a major conceptual error because if human identity comes in two genders—"is born a twin"—then a combination of the two perceptions may be necessary for our survival. In my book *Green Paradise Lost* I say that I think we are rushing into the future with one eye closed. It is like trying to see three-dimensionally with one eye closed. You cannot. It is like trying to hear music in stereo with one ear closed. You cannot. It is interesting, then, that we were created with two ears and two eyes—and that the human species was created in both male and female versions.

I am convinced that there is evolutionary knowledge encoded in the female of the human species, and that one of the worst things patriarchy has done is lock up that knowledge encoded there and exclude it from the realm of public life and discourse. Let me give you one brief example. Some years ago I learned, after it had happened, about an interesting lecture my daughter had given to my teenage son. My daughter was in college and my teenage son was away at school nearby. He had decided while off on his first weekend away to take an extra day with his then-girl friend and not tell the school. When he returned he asked his sister to pick him up at the train station and drive him to school.

"Hunter," she said, "I know that when you are away with a girl on a weekend like this, you can't imagine the consequences of your not coming back. And I'm not talking about the fits that the administration had or the fact that you missed Monday's classes. I am really concerned that you didn't start writing your term paper. Don't you understand that even though you think those consequences are far away from you, remote, you *are* going to reach them in time?" She went on. "Let me tell you how I discovered that. I discovered it because I realized that nine months down the road from any sexual encounter I, as a woman, am likely going to bear the consequences of that sexual encounter."

I think that is very interesting *woman*-learning. From my work at the Sloan School of Management I can tell you that when you get into some of the most sophisticated analyses of today's culture, one of the most prominent problems we encounter is that there is no adequate concern for the long-term future. The focus is repeatedly on making immediate decisions for what will have benefits right away. One part of the current critique of why American corporate management is not doing as good a job of managing as are their Japanese and German counterparts is that European and Japanese management do not make investment decisions and evaluate corporate performance on the basis of financial or sales results this quarter-year, but with the next half-decade or decade in mind. You must understand that there is nothing in the biological experience of the male to convince him that nine months (or a half-decade or decade) hence he will experience the consequences of something done today—and that those consequences will decisively shape his life for a generation. But that sort of knowledge is encoded

33

in the female of the species, and by junior or senior high my daughter knew that and had translated this learning into the realization that two months from now you are going to hate yourself for not starting to write that term paper on time.

It turns out that there is also a great deal of difference between the way the males of the species react to risk and the way females do. It should be no news to anyone that males tend to prove their masculinity by taking risks. Females, on the other hand, are risk-averse, perhaps because for all kinds of reasons they are used to nurturing their brood. Who really knows why? But it turns out that, for example, the more you tell women about nuclear technology, including nuclear energy, the less they want it. Lecturing around the country I have had interesting things said to me that further confirm this. Once I told a gathering that a sociologist had observed that environmental conservation is considered feminine, whereas high-risk technologies are considered masculine. A male student confirmed this, saying that he had just completed a summer's apprenticeship and it was interesting because, among the males, nobody wanted to work on passive solar energy; everybody wanted to work on active solar! So these male and female tendencies are pervasive. We are kidding ourselves if we think that we do not need the knowledge and the alternative experience and perspective that are available only when we are seeing with both eyes. There is no way of seeing the future in three dimensions without using both eyes, both genders.

The Other Great Conceptual Error

Then there is the other great conceptual mistake, the way in which we have imaged or seen ourselves and our place on planet Earth. Here we are talking about what Walter Lippmann called "the picture in our minds of the world beyond our reach." And what are they? I think the easiest way to visualize this is to close one's eyes and listen to the world as it is described in Psalm 8:4–6:

> What is man that thou art mindful of him? . . .
> Yet thou hast made him little less than God, . . .
> Thou hast put all things under his feet.

In a little snapshot you have there a view of "the picture in our mind of the world beyond our reach" that says life is hierarchical. Life is a pyramid of values. Life is a ladder in which that which is of more value is *up* and that which is of lesser value is farther *down*. (See Figure 1.) We are implicitly told by this picture (what in the Middle Ages was called The Great Chain of Being) that "that's the way reality is, folks."

The illustration shown in Figure 2 was commissioned by the Education Development Center when it was doing curriculum about the Hebrew Bible (Old Testament). The caption was based on Genesis texts: "The people of the Old Testament believed in only one God who had created a divine order and placed people above nature. He gave people dominion over the fish of the sea, over the fowl of the air, over the cattle, and over all the earth." You can see the hand of God putting the divine order in place and blessing it, and humans are at the top of the pyramid and everything else is below.

Recall what I said earlier about white/black mythology and the relationship between what is thought and who the people are who end up benefiting from that way of thinking. Now we, female as well as male, have all been socialized to accept this up/down picture of the world as a hierarchically organized universe. That is what we have learned to think is reality. God is "above," "spirit" is of most value and is always "up." I once went through our hymnal and found a total of three hymns that did not do the "spirit-is-up" and "come-down-upon-us" thing. Up-and-downness is absolutely crucial to the way we think about God.

Men are below God, and women below men. If we think that is not true, listen to these words of great thinkers from our past (Bowman 28ff.). Today we cannot even imagine anyone saying such things about women, but we are the inheritors of this intellectual and theological tradition. It begins with Aristotle: "A female is a female by virtue of a certain lack of qualities, a

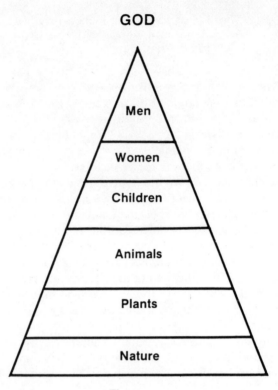

GOD

Men

Women

Children

Animals

Plants

Nature

Figure I

natural defectiveness." If you wonder what that means, let me tell you about a woman who studied in India and Thailand for more than a decade and became the first woman to become a genuine Buddhist master. She did all this without any feminist awareness. She became feminist after she had become a Buddhist master, and she discovered such things as that there are relevant qualities necessary to be a Buddha—and the eleventh is an "unsheathed penis." So, we are not talking about quaint things; what it really comes down to is a woman does not have a penis. What is male is right, it is normative, and not to have a penis is to be defective, to depart from the essential criteria, the essential qualities of the *spiritual* norm required of Buddhas.

Tertullian, near the end of the second century of the Christian

Reprinted by permission of The Education Development Center

Figure 2

era, wrote: "Do you know that each of you women is an Eve? The sentence of God—on this sex of yours—lives in this age; the guilt must necessarily live, too. You are the Gate of Hell, you are the temptress of the forbidden tree; you are the first deserter of the divine law." If you think those views are outmoded, consider Woody Allen's movie *Interiors,* in which the children are mentally ill, the father's name is Adam, and his first wife (whom they all blame for their condition) is, you guessed it, named Eve! Or again, several years ago, the Southern Baptists' national legislative convention decided that no women can be ordained as ministers because women are descendants of Eve, sin came into the world with women, and therefore women today cannot be ministers.

In A.D. 584 in Lyons, France, forty-three Christian bishops and twenty men representing other bishops held a most peculiar debate: "Are Women Human?" After lengthy arguments a vote was taken. The results were thirty-two yes, thirty-one no. Women were declared human by *one vote* in the sixth century of the Christian tradition!

In the mid-nineteenth century the Protestant theologian Soren Kierkegaard wrote: "What a misfortune to be a woman. And yet, the worst misfortune is not to understand what a misfortune it is." Karl Barth, perhaps the major Protestant theologian of the twentieth century, claims that woman is *ontologically subordinate to man.*

We women have been living with all this. Women have been conceptualized as inferior to the normative male. Children are below women. Just as for a long time it was felt that men "owned" women. Today we still feel that we own our children. The reason we cannot get a handle on child abuse is because the state, the neighbors, the police, all kinds of people hesitate to intervene. A fourteen-year-old boy in Dayton, Ohio, shot his father, a father who was abusing the entire family. The neighbors knew it was an abuse case; the school apparently knew. But we feel that we cannot move in such cases because we still think adults "own" children. I now look back on the biblical story of Abraham and Isaac (Genesis 22), and I realize that if God had not stopped Abraham from killing Isaac, Abraham would not have been prosecuted for either child abuse or murder. Patriarchal men had the power of life and death over all their properties: not only land and dwelling and trees and animals, but also women, slaves, concubines, and children.

We call animals and plants subhuman species. We feel free to torture hundreds of thousands of animals every year in medical and commercial research in order to bring some medical good to our own species. We rarely ask ourselves if this is ethically or morally right. Never, because they are below us. And therefore, why shouldn't a thousand of them offer their lives in pain if we can bring one small medical advance to the human species? We do not even question such work, just as men for so long did not question what they did to women. Plants we do not identify with at all. We can imagine the pain of animals but not the pain of plants. Plants are clearly below animals in the hierarchy of being. And nature is at the bottom.

This is a *command* hierarchy, and the illusion is that God tells us what to do, we tell others, and others obey. The illusion here is that you can be at some standing point and from there rank diversity, rank God-given diversity within what we are now finally beginning to comprehend in an alternative way as a nonhierarchical and extremely interactive system. But we have thought that we could stand at some magical standing point and say, "*This* is superior to this" and "*That* is below that." The intellectual arrogance in this is incredible. One thing I learned studying ecology is that diversity is essential to the well-being and stability of the natural systems God has created. But within patriarchy we have never been able to value such diversity, so we rank it; and then we expect that which we say is "below" to *obey* that which we say is "above."

All through the Middle Ages and the Enlightenment this hierarchy of ranking was called The Great Chain of Being. Then, in the mid-1800s, Darwin said that we are *descended* from animals. His next-to-last book was entitled *The Descent of Man*. That was like dropping humans (males) three or four levels in the cosmic caste system we had created for ourselves. Christian leaders, as well as lay people, did not like that idea one bit, and Darwin knew they would not. He had been trained in theology at Cambridge, and he wanted nothing to do with the heat and the controversy his theory of evolution was sure to stir up.

39

Charles Darwin's theory of evolution was at first widely rejected. But a century later, when we had had time to domesticate it, Jacob Bronowski could entitle his book and subsequent television series *The Ascent of Man*. We could forget the divine hand blessing and creating; we could forget about "spirit" and the very top of the pyramid of being. What evolutionary theory offered was not a creation from "above," but an evolution from below, out of the primeval soup through the "lower" species and finally to us, homo sapiens, at the top of the evolutionary process. Why do we speak of "lower" species? Because *they* are simple and *we* are complex. The assumption, of course, is that complexity is of more value than simplicity. Because we think that we are complex, we think that complexity is of great value. So what we have done in evolutionary theory for those who do not want to incorporate God into evolution is to lop off the top of the pyramid of life. But the evolutionary pyramid without God is still the same cosmic caste structure that earlier The Great Chain of Being had projected onto the cosmos, and thus legitimated as the way things are.

In the popular grasp of evolution we have confused human uniqueness with superiority. Any biologist will tell you that all species are unique. That is *not* to deny that human beings are unique and do some things that are one of a kind, unique. But we never think to ask ourselves which species can run fastest because it is not us. We never ask which species has the best eyesight because it is not us. We never ask which species has the best hearing because it is not us. We never ask which species has the best sense of smell, again, because it is not us. When I take my son's Siberian husky for a walk, it is clear how minimal our skills are in the world of smells. Every three steps our husky experiences orgasms of delight by simply smelling a bush, while I do not smell a thing!

We said for a time that the best species had the biggest brain because *we* thought that was *us*. Now we have discovered that whales and dolphins have just as large brains as we do, and probably they have just as developed styles of thought even though they live out their lives in a watery world. We never asked ourselves whether what humans do is as spectacular and

40

important for the life of the planet as what plants do in photosynthesis because I am not sure we could say yes. So instead we never asked the question!

If you can talk to people about why they are convinced we are so much better than animals, they say, "Because we can kill more of them than they can kill of us." That is an interesting hypothesis. If that were true, then the Nazis, because they killed so many in the Holocaust, would indeed have been the superior species they claimed to be.

Ranking Diversity

The ranking of diversity began very early, when man looked at woman and asked, "Which of us is better?" From so simple a beginning we have, all of us, been deeply socialized to rank diversities of all kinds. Humans look at trees and ask, "Which of us is better?" Whites look at blacks and ask, "Which of us is better?" Civilized look at so-called primitives and ask, "Which of us is better?"

In the ecological perspective this is a most ridiculous question. Diversity exists on this planet so different things get done. Because different things need to be done, and there is no distinction between little and big things that need doing, diversity itself has ecological value: it helps life. But unfortunately diversity is ranked in our culture, and it can be argued that this habit of mind stems from the distinctions and ranking between males and females that pervade patriarchal culture and its institutions from our earliest times.

So we need to finish the Copernican revolution. We started out thinking that we were at the center of the cosmos and that the sun, the moon, and the stars revolved around us. Then we discovered that this astronomy of the heavens was not true and, with difficulty, we redid our anthropocentric astronomy. You'll recall that the Christian church did not like Copernicus and Galileo then any more than later it liked Darwin and his ideas. But while we were changing our sense of the heavens—our astronomy—we left firmly in place the cosmic hierarchy—our gut conviction that we humans are above the rest of nature.

The ranking of diversity is always a basis of oppression. It is not accidental that the Nazis, in order to do to the Jews what they did, had to convince themselves that the Jews were sub-human. It is not accidental that in order for whites to do to blacks what was done in slavery, whites came up with an elaborate rationale based on the Old Testament to prove that blacks are inferior. And we are still calling animals subhuman, so we do not question what we do to them. Such ranking of diversity *always* legitimates oppression.

These are some of the reasons we need to revisit and reassess the Garden of Eden and its place in our religious and cultural heritage. The Garden has been an important organizing symbol around which much has clustered that we now have to label as a "bad dream," a not-helpful mythology about ourselves and the earth. What we need to do now, for our own sake and for the earth's sake, is to reimagine, reconceptualize, even re-mythologize, our place on the planet Earth.

Reassessing the Garden View

Take still another look at the Genesis story of the old Garden of Eden. Notice that in the Adam and Eve story, *woman* is born out of the male body, despite the fact that in real life both males and females are born out of women's bodies. The Genesis account turns that upside down, reverses it. Genesis also says unambiguously that woman is created to be a helpmate to man. (There is nothing about each being created to be the helpmate of the other.) The biblical scholar B. Davie Napier, in his poetic restatement of the Genesis stories and themes for our own day, *Come Sweet Death,* does a profound but humorous piece about Adam's awareness that Eve was created "for him," to satisfy *his* desire, to complement *his* life, and to make *his* life better. Similar views continue to cause problems between males and females as they struggle in our own day to conceptualize their lives and their relationships centuries after Genesis.

In the biblical account there is no death inside the Garden.

Death in this account is a celestial zap, a punishment for sin that is visited on us only after we leave the Garden. This also is not true to human experience.

A huge doctrine of original sin has also been constructed through the Christian centuries on the simple Garden of Eden story. Jewish scholars in our own day look at this Christian doctrine of original sin and the "fall" and ask, "Where do they get all of that?" The biblical account just says that humans were sent out of the Garden (Genesis 3:23). The words "fall" and "original sin" do not appear in the text. They and the doctrines associated with them are something later, a construct added long afterward.

But when today someone talks about moving beyond war, the Garden of Eden and "original sin" are invoked, always to undercut such ameliorative aspirations and label them as unrealistic and utopian. We are told that back there in the Garden it was possible not to have war, not to have slavery. But man sinned, and because of sin we will always have war, we will always have slavery, we will always have violence. We cannot (we are told) move toward a more harmonious society *because* of human sinfulness.

This deeply jaded view of our (sinful) human nature lies behind a recent cartoon showing Earth in the shape of a rotting tomato. On top of this disintegrating planet a father and son stand, and the father, in the caption, is saying, "My boy, some day none of this will be yours." The cartoonist is assuming the human father's illusion of his own dominion—that he owns the planet and he can pass it on to his son—and at the same time ridiculing this in the light of current ecological devastation resulting from that human sense of dominion. But isn't it interesting that not even on the planet or anywhere in the picture is the woman who gave birth to and probably largely raised the son. She is invisible in all this.

The Pervasive Maleness

The patriarchal tradition has projected this same pervasive maleness onto God. God, in our tradition, is imaged as a male God, a King, a Father, a Lord. In this framework of thought and its resulting institutions God is one to be obeyed. It is a tradition obsessed with patriarchal issues of its own authority, its own power, and these now projected onto the cosmos as the essential requirements God has of us. The required human stance is seen as one of obedience and belief, and God is perceived as the source of unchanging order, as Father, as King, as the Ultimate Word and Judge.

Peter Berger, in *The Sacred Canopy*, points out that religion legitimates social institutions by bestowing on them an ultimately valid ontological status, by locating them within a sacred and cosmic frame of reference. The feminist theologian Mary Daly said it more succinctly: "When God is male, the male is God." What the maleness of God does is legitimate not only the patriarchal society, but also the image of the patriarchal home in which the man is "king of the castle"; the woman is "wife," doing her domestic chores of rearing children, washing dishes, and getting meals; and the child is being obedient. The really important issue in the patriarchal family, as in the patriarchal society and patriarchal church, is control.

Many people would like to move us back to homes in which children obey, in which women are "at home" and doing "their" jobs, and in which "Dad" (or Father) is calling the shots. But we also need to be clear that the system of patriarchal families had a lot of child abuse and wife battering and an incredible amount of incest. The latest figures are that one out of every four women has been sexually molested in her childhood, and one out of ten men were sexually molested as young boys. Male figures (fathers, grandfathers, stepfathers, uncles, brothers) have done the majority of this sexual molesting.[2] In prisons today a high percentage of men who committed violent crimes were sexually molested in their childhood. All this has been hidden. When all this was beyond the closed doors and drawn curtains of the obedient mind in the patriarchal home, then you could not talk about being an incest victim, you could not talk about marital rape or being a battered wife. All this is just now beginning to come out and be disclosed as skeletons that have been kept hidden in the patriarchal closet by the enforced obedience and silence of wives and children.

The New Garden That Is Emerging

Our generation has the incredible opportunity and privilege of understanding God's creation not only through the biblical accounts and biblical tradition, but also through the perceptions, new in this century, of modern physics and ecology.

Astrophysics has helped us to realize that we live on a planet in a solar system in the galaxy of the Milky Way within a universe that consists of 193 billion such galaxies. I keep thinking of J. B. Phillips' book title *Your God Is Too Small*. None of us has any adequate ideas of a God that is creating 193 billion galaxies. That's the very big, the macro dimension of our creation context. In the very small, the micro dimension of our creation context, those who work in subatomic physics are helping us to see that we are, all of us, connected in the probability patterns of energy that flow through everything equally, through humans, cats, animals, plants, trees, butterflies, everything. What we now discern at the micro level of the very small is a pervasive pattern of subatomic energy moving through absolutely everything.

In between the very big and the very small is the everyday dimension of our creation context. Here it is becoming evident that, far from being able to bend nature to do our every whim, we are confronted with a planet that has restrictions, limits. The planet, too, is limited in energy resources, in oil and coal and natural gas and uranium reserves. It is also limited in the quantities and locations of metallic ores that are economically or politically or technologically feasible to mine. And of course each of us personally, far from having dominion over Earth, has only a limited length of time, our lifetime, that we can dwell on it. Each of these limits of our finite planet is like the biblical angel with the flaming sword in the old Garden of Eden story in Genesis (Genesis 3:24). If we cannot live accommodating to these limits of our current Garden, we will be more abruptly thrown out and exiled from it.

The wrong thing in our thinking about the old Garden of Eden story is our thinking that it is a story about some past. The only such garden we will ever know is this beautiful, green, and fragile planet. If we do not live within its various limits, those

45

limits are going to throw us out. One or more of these limits will kill us right here—in the smog, or the toxic wastes, or the cancers, or by radiation poisoning, or nuclear war. We will then have reenacted, in a terrible and modern way, the Garden of Eden story. Our alternative is to rethink our role in the Garden, to reconceptualize our sense of place on this planet.

The Ecology of the New Garden of Eden

Our planet, our world, is a complex web or system of interconnections. That is what ecology, as a biological discipline, helps us to understand. We live within the biosphere, a four-mile-deep membrane of life over the surface of Earth. Within the biosphere are all the biological life-support systems that keep alive everything that is alive on the planet. What is our place in this biosphere? It is certainly not the old place of command and dominion. If you remember Dr. Seuss' book for children, *Horton Hears a Who,* we humans on this planet are like tiny Whos living invisibly in the fuzz of a tennis ball, and that tennis ball is our Earth. The fuzz on the ball is the biosphere that keeps us, and all life, alive. (See Table 1.)

We should teach our children that when God created the world, God created the life-supporting cycles of the biosphere. We live within these cycles and they flow through our lungs, our veins, our guts. The water cycle, the carbon cycle, the oxygen cycle—what is important to realize is that all these cycles move in circles. They cycle and recycle materials again and again. One part of the cycle takes in raw materials, does its thing, and then produces waste products. But there is no waste in the miracle of these cycles. Each waste product is just what some other part of the cycle needs as raw material (or "food"). Each part of the cycle then comes around and dumps its particular by-product or waste, which is just what another part of the cycle needs. These cycles are powered by the energy of the sun, and they will go on indefinitely as long as the sun continues to shine.

One such cycle is the oxygen cycle, in which plants, as a by-product of their photosynthesis, breathe out the oxygen that fish, insects, animals, and also human beings need. We all

Table 1

1. *Energy Cycle of the Earth*—solar energy coming in, being circulated by the atmosphere and oceans, and finally being radiated back out into space
2. *Energy Cycle of the Biosphere*—solar energy being converted by photosynthesis in green plants into complex carbohydrates
3. *Water Cycle*—the transportation system of the life processes
4. *Carbon Cycle*—CO_2—living matter—CO_2
5. *Oxygen Cycle*—starts from photosynthesis in plants and makes animal, fish, and insect life possible
6. *Nitrogen Cycle*—79% of Earth's atmosphere; "fixed" by special organisms or industrial processes so it can be used by living things
7. *Mineral Cycles*—especially phosphorus and sulfur; especially the carboxylation cycle, the soluble (i.e., not volatile)-element cycle, and eutrophication
8. *Human Energy Production*
9. *Human Food Production*
10. *Human Materials Production*

Source: G. Evelyn Hutchinson, "The Biosphere," *Scientific American* 22 (Sept. 1970):45–53.

breathe in oxygen, use it to oxidize and release the energy stored in our foods so our bodies can have access to it, and we then breathe back to the plants the carbon dioxide they need to breathe in. Did you know that oxygen is not just somehow "out there" in the atmosphere of our planet? There is oxygen here at all only because it has been breathed out by green plants of the ocean or the forests or the grassland plains. When we kill enough of the trees and plants and tropical rain forests and photoplankton in the oceans, there will be insufficient oxygen for all of us to breathe.

There was a time early in Earth's natural history when there was not enough oxygen in the atmosphere for fish and insects and animals and humans to develop. Only as green plants greatly increased in numbers, and thus oxygen increased, could the evolution of nonplant species get underway. Evolution is an interconnected process, just as life today on the planet is. It is a

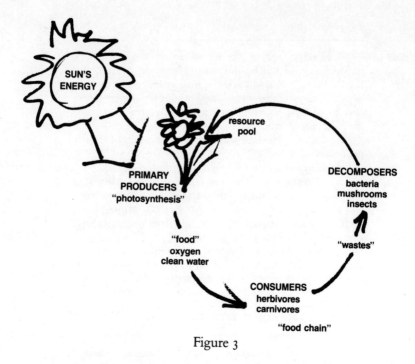

SUN'S ENERGY

PRIMARY
PRODUCERS
"photosynthesis"

resource
pool

DECOMPOSERS
bacteria
mushrooms
insects

"food"
oxygen
clean water

"wastes"

CONSUMERS
herbivores
carnivores

"food chain"

Figure 3

system of ecosystems, and in the mystery of God's wonderfulness it all fits together, using wastes and supporting life
(including human life). It is all powered by the energy of the sun
and, wonder of wonders, it manages itself! No degrees in
business administration are required. It functions totally without
government subsidies! The biosphere and *life* are truly mirac-
ulous.

The Circle of Life

In the new Garden of Eden we can better think of *the circle of life*
than of a hierarchical pyramid. Life's processes are not a cosmic
caste system of control and obedience as suggested in Psalm 8
and the "dominion" model of our place on the planet. (See
Figure 3.) As long as the sun continues to shine, the "primary
producer" on the planet is the plants. The photosynthesis of

plants is the absolute basis of all other life. Plants take in simple molecules and convert them into complex molecules ("food"), oxygen, and clean water. "Consumers" feed on plants and on one another in what is called the "food chain." The food chain really is a hierarchy. In it the larger feed on the smaller. Humans have conceptualized this hierarchy as a pyramid with us on top because we eat them and they do not eat us. We, in our wonderfulness, think that makes us what we call "top carnivore." But ecologists point out that our view of the pyramid is upside down and that we are at the bottom of the food chain; *we need* the whole rest of the pyramid and they do not need us. We are expendable. If the photoplankton go, the whole food chain in the ocean fisheries will collapse, and we as "top carnivore," the ultimate consumer, are the most vulnerable.

All "consumers"—all animals, fish, insects, and us—produce what, from our viewpoint, are wastes, and the "decomposers"— the mushrooms, insects, and bacteria—decompose these wastes and produce the simple molecules stripped of virtually all energy. These simple molecules make up the resource pool that plants as "producers" draw on again and again. We must understand how indebted we and all life on this planet are to these decomposers. If everything that had ever lived on the planet were still here, what a mess and stink that would be! Rejoice, then, that in the new Eden we can appreciate that the small-to-invisible decomposers are always at work transforming and recycling us, our bodies, our wastes, our garbage.

Contrast this circle of life, which will go on as long as the sun shines, with industrial systems that humans have created. (See Figure 4.) The problem here is not capitalism, or for that matter socialism or communism. These are economic arrangements that, for all their differences, are still based on industrial systems of production. What industrial systems produce in goods and services is measured in dollars and aggregated as gross national product, or GNP. What the biosphere, through the circle of life, produces goes largely unmeasured in dollars and could be termed the gross biological production. The global biological production is orders of magnitude (10 or 100 or 1,000 times) larger than the global industrial production.

From Figure 4 it is clear that an industrial system of produc-

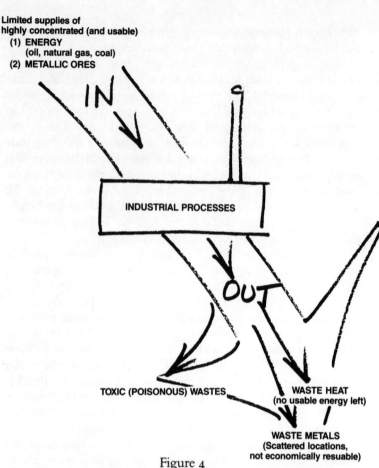

Figure 4

Limited capacities of the planet's ability to absorb, decompose, or otherwise recycle industrial wastes

tion that draws on limited resources of highly concentrated energy and metallic ores is not indefinitely sustainable. Likewise, its production is finally destined for the various garbage or scrap heaps of the world, so that its wastes are not the sources of new inputs to the industrial system; they are simply wastes, useless and unusable by the industrial system for any economic purpose. Likewise, the vast quantities of waste heat poured into rivers, oceans, and airways have no further economic use to the industrial system, and indeed the biological systems have limited capacities to absorb and dissipate so much heat. The toxic wastes, while smaller in volume, similarly overwhelm the capacities of rivers, oceans, and atmospheres to deal with them, and those biological resources are degraded (polluted) and changed by their presence.

The circular character of biological cycles is indefinitely sustainable. The linear character of industrial "throughput" is definitely not sustainable and cuts across the biospheral processes on which we and all life are absolutely dependent. The technologies on which our industrial system is based are not attuned to using the sun's energy except in the form of geologically preserved fossil fuels. Nor are these technologies adapted to raw materials that the biosphere is continually producing in such abundance. Instead, the industrial system gobbles up low-entropy (concentrated and easily usable) energy and metallic ores that we extract from Earth's crust with the illusion that there will always be more.

But there won't *be* more! These fossil fuels and ore deposits are an accumulation made over aeons of geological time. They are depletable resources, and we are depleting them rapidly, using them up "as though there were no tomorrow." Then the industrial system throws out, discards high-entropy (unusable) clutter or waste, along with vast amounts of low-grade, unusable waste heat and lesser, but still significant quantities of various toxic (poisonous) substances. We think all this can go on for a long time, but we do not ask how long. We and our industrial system of production are but a blip—a transient phenomenon—in the geological history of Earth. We and our industrial system as it is today will soon be gone.

Rebuilding the Garden

The task that lies before us is to redesign the technologies of our current linear model of industrial production so that they fit more and more within the cycles of the biosphere, within the circle of life. These technologies must harvest energies that are renewed daily. They must function so that wastes become resources for other processes. They must be made to fit productively and harmoniously inside the biospheral processes of production without destroying them. We can see the problem, as well as the possibilities for change, most clearly when we consider the modern industrial model of agricultural production. Fossil fuel-powered machinery, as well as fertilizers and pesticides and biocides fabricated in energy-intensive processes from fossil fuels, as well as farming practices that erode the millennia-old accumulations of fine soil, simply do not constitute a sustainable agricultural system. Alternative farming practices and technologies are now being fashioned to return more productive farmers to sustainable farms and farm life.

We exist on this planet not in dominion, but like fetuses. We are totally dependent on this planet for all the functions essential to our living. Those biospheral cycles hold us in life; they bring us our clean air and food and water, and they take away our wastes, just as the placenta in the mother's body does for the fetus. We are in no position of dominion here. There is no way you can be a fetus and realistically think you have dominion over the whole life-process. If you nevertheless should think that you have dominion and act that way, you are like the person who jumped off the top of the skyscraper and, falling past someone looking out at the twentieth floor, shouted to the observer, "So far, so good!" That person has not crashed yet, but certainly the prospects are, to say the least, limited. The future prospects of the dominion view of our human place on Earth are "limited."

The Covenant Given Us in the Garden

We are alive within a system that is interconnected. A system, simply defined, is something in which everything affects everything else. We are just beginning to understand what it means to live in a system of interconnectedness. We are so enormously interconnected that it is awe-inspiring. Consider the case of the Antarctic penguins. There have never been insects in Antarctica because of its climate. Hence DDT was never used there. But there is DDT in the body tissues of the penguins of Antarctica (as there is in the body tissues of every living thing sampled).

How did the DDT get to the penguins, through snow and the oceans and the food chain?[3]

This Earth is now our Garden. It is a system with this extraordinary interrelatedness. This Earth, this Garden, is what God created and has set us in the midst of. This interrelatedness is the real covenant given us in the creation. Now, in the light of all this, let us talk about God. Even as we reconceptualize life in this Garden, we must also be reconceptualizing how we think about God.

I think God is an incredible Mystery. However we may choose to name that Mystery—divine presence, ground of being (Tillich), ultimate reality, creative process—any of these images or words are things that *we,* in our human wonderfulness, dream up and that *we* then throw out at that ontological Mystery and say, How did you like that description? These descriptions of ours have absolutely nothing to do with the actual nature of what that Mystery is. And the Mystery is not at all disturbed if we say, "We'll take back a few, such as 'God-the-Father,' and we'll throw up a few new ones to see if they are a little better match to all your mysteriousness."

With theologian Paul Tillich, let us take a closer look at how we use finite words or symbols to signify to ourselves what is infinite. Tillich has said that if we choose a symbol like Father, we not only bring God down, but also give a great boost to the status of the institution of fatherhood because our chosen symbol subtly suggests that fatherhood is somehow God-like. We have begun to deify the human institution of fatherhood (Tillich 204ff.).

I do not know what it means to call God either father or mother, either male or female. This is because I do not know what it means to say male or female without talking also about genitals. I do not think that the ultimate Mystery of the universe has genitals. Theologians say that, of course, they know that God has no genitals. But if that is so and they know it, then why do male theologians get so upset at the idea of imaging God as female after so many centuries of imaging God as male?

I would like to use other images to suggest God as the ultimate creative Mystery of the universe. I would like to use images that do not "boost" any human beings or castes or institutions into borrowed status or power or privilege because they are somehow, in some attribute, "god-like." I want instead to suggest that we use some of the images we are getting as clues from astronomy and subatomic physics and ecology, and use these as new metaphors or images about God. We might all be better served by such new images.

Other Images of God

Here are a few possibilities. God is the "power of relationship," as in an ecological *web*. We live in a totally interconnected system, and the truth is that we would disintegrate in the life system without such things as gravity, electromagnetic fields, without all that holds both planets and electrons, the very large and very small, in their orbits. In a recent book, *The Redemption of God,* Carter Heyward speaks of God as "the power of relationship itself" (172). We are not talking simply human relationships, we are talking all sorts of relationships—everything! Physicist Brian Swimme, in *The Universe Is a Green Dragon,* talks about the power of "allurement." Allurement is gravity and electromagnetic fields, what holds planets in orbit. God, then, in all these ways and more, is the power of relationship.

Life in the universe is also an incredible process of "flow." We may name as *flame* what we see atop a candle, but a flame is not an object, but a flow. A flame is never the same, for it is always burning, oxidizing the newly melting wax or oil or other fuel, always the same yet new. A waterfall is a similar phenomenon. We name one Niagara Falls, but the water going over the brink in that same configuration and shape is always new water and always changing. A cloud is like this too. We give these phenomena—a candle, a waterfall, a cloud—names as though they were simple objects, but what we are naming is actually an identifiable and continuing flow or process.

You and I personally are also a flow, albeit a slower-moving flow. There are always some of our atoms that were long ago in the flesh of dinosaurs or in primitive oceans. Physiologically we are a continual flow, a process of taking in, reconstituting, and giving out of air, of food and wastes, and finally our bodies are a flow as they grow and age and continually renew themselves until finally we die. In this context, then, how about God as "the power of transformation"—what keeps that flow or process of transformation moving and yet distinctively shaped? God is the power of transformation that moves awesomely in you, in me, and in this universe of 193 billion galaxies and is continually transforming *everything* from what it has been and is now into what it will be!

Because light and sound, like your heart and life, have a beat, I have thought also about God as "the *pulse* of life in the universe." George Leonard, in *The Silent Pulse,* talks about the extent to which much of reality in the world is a vibration, a resonance phenomenon. God is the pulse that keeps everything not only in place, but also resonating, moving, and continually transformed and new.

More than we have ever perceived we live in a universe of incredible Shine, Shimmer, and Dance. Our eyes at many points have been blinded to the wonder of it. We have not honored the diversity in creation because we have been preoccupied with ranking it into cosmic caste systems of greater and lesser value and worth.

Now the new perceiving eyes of physics and ecology—like trumpet flourishes announcing entrance into the royal presence—have given us radically new eyes to see the reality of this Shining, this Shimmering, this Dancing. What I invite you now to do is take off your hierarchical-ranking eyeglasses and put aside your patriarchal vision so that we may all join with other species and come inside the circle of creation, and join the great dance.

Notes

1. United Nations Commission on the Status of Women, *Newsletter* 3 (1980) (UN Decade for Women, Copenhagen Conference, 1980). See also Lisa Leghorn and Katherine Parker, *Woman's Worth: Sexual Economics and the World of Women* (Boston: Routledge & Kegan Paul, 1981).

2. Judith Lewis Herman, *Father-Daughter Incest* (Cambridge, MA:

Harvard University Press, 1981). See also Toni A.H. McNaron and Yarrow Morgan, eds., *Voices in the Night: Women Speaking About Incest* (Pittsburgh: Cleis Press, 1982), for accounts by daughters who were incest victims of their own families.

3. W.T.L. Sladen, C.M. Menzee, and W.L. Rechel, "DDT Residues in Adelie Penguins and a Crabeater Seal from Antarctica," *Nature* 210 (1966):670–73; R.W. Risebrough et al., "Transfer of Chlorinated Biphenyls to Antarctica," *Nature* 264 (1976):738–39. Cited by Paul R. Ehrlich, Anne H. Ehrlich, and John P. Holdren, *Ecoscience: Population, Resources, Environment* (San Francisco: W. H. Freeman, 1977).

Works Cited

Berger, Peter L. *The Sacred Canopy: Elements of a Sociological Theory of Religion*. Garden City, NY: Doubleday, 1967.

————, and Thomas Luckmann. *The Social Construction of Reality: A Treatise in the Sociology of Knowledge*. Garden City, NY: Anchor Books, 1967.

Bowman, Meg. "Why We Burn: Sexism Exorcised." *Humanist*, Nov.-Dec. 1983, 28ff.

Bronowski, Jacob. *The Ascent of Man*. Boston: Little, Brown, 1973.

Ehrlich, Paul R., Anne H. Ehrlich, and John P. Holdren. *Ecoscience: Population, Resources, Environment*. San Francisco: W. H. Freeman, 1977.

Gilligan, Carol. *In a Different Voice: Psychological Theory and Women's Development*. Cambridge, MA: Harvard University Press, 1982.

Gray, Elizabeth Dodson. *Green Paradise Lost*. Wellesley, MA: Roundtable Press, 1979.

————. *Patriarchy as a Conceptual Trap*. Wellesley, MA: Roundtable Press, 1982.

Herman, Judith Lewis. *Father-Daughter Incest*. Cambridge, MA: Harvard University Press, 1981.

Heyward, Isabel Carter. *The Redemption of God: A Theology of Mutual Relation*. Lanham, MD: University Press of America, 1982.

Hutchinson, G. Evelyn. "The Biosphere." *Scientific American* 223 (Sept. 1970):45–53.

Kohlberg, Lawrence. *The Philosophy of Moral Development: Essays in Moral Development*, vol. 1. New York: Harper & Row, 1981.

Leghorn, Lisa, and Katherine Parker. *Woman's Worth: Sexual Economics and the World of Women*. Boston: Routledge & Kegan Paul, 1981.

Leonard, George. *The Silent Pulse: A Search for the Perfect Rhythm That Exists in Each of Us*. New York: E. P. Dutton, 1978.

Lippmann, Walter. *Public Opinion.* New York: Macmillan, 1922.

McNaron, Toni A. H., and Yarrow Morgan, eds. *Voices in the Night: Women Speaking About Incest.* Pittsburgh: Cleis Press, 1982.

Napier, B. Davie. *Come Sweet Death: A Quintet from Genesis.* New York: The Pilgrim Press, 1967.

Risebrough, R. W., et al. "Transfer of Chlorinated Biphenyls to Antarctica." *Nature 264 (1976):738–39.*

Sladen, W. T. L., C. M. Menzee, and W. L. Rechel. "DDT Residues in Adelie Penguins and a Crabeater Seal from Antarctica." *Nature* 210 (1966):670–73.

Swimme, Brian. *The Universe Is a Green Dragon: A Cosmic Creation Story.* Santa Fe, NM: Bear, 1985.

Tillich, Paul. *Systematic Theology,* vol. 1. Chicago: University of Chicago Press, 1951.

United Nations Commission on the Status of Women. *Newsletter* 3 (1980).

CHAPTER 3

Do Women Have a History?

Reassessing the Past and Present

ANN J. LANE

A Personal Journey

WHEN I WAS a graduate student at Columbia University in the late 1950s, I studied Early American History with Dumas Malone. He was a venerable and venerated Jeffersonian scholar, deservedly so, a gentle, sweet man, close to retirement, and his students suspected that sometimes he forgot who was Malone and who was Jefferson, so immersed in his work was he. He was seen one Sunday morning on Morningside Drive, approaching the campus, with two tomes weighing him down, one under each arm, one of Jefferson and one of Hamilton. "Why, Professor Malone, even on Sunday?" asked an eager student, himself on the way to the library. "Oh," said the eminent gentleman, beaming with pride, "Sunday is my day with the Great Men."

I tell that anecdote because it evokes for me how tickled I was at the time, how grand it felt to be in that world, if only the margin of it, to absorb the intoxicating intellectual air of a university life in which one cavorted with the likes of Thomas Jefferson and Alexander Hamilton. I had some problems with Jefferson because he was a slaveowner and the author of a book asserting the racial inferiority of blacks. And I had some problems with Hamilton because he was personally and politically a scoundrel. But it never occurred to me then that I should have some problems identifying with them because they were men. I could have imagined no tomes of women's writings to cart to my office on a Sunday in 1956. It never occurred to me to look because I was in the company of important folks. I, too, would someday carry tomes of Jefferson and Hamilton under my arms as I made my way to my office at Columbia University.

As I look back to understand my own odyssey, my own journey from that time to this, it becomes clear that my life altered significantly when I began to work on a book about a woman named Mary Ritter Beard.

In 1946 she wrote a book called *Woman as Force in History.* I went to college in the 1950s and then on to graduate school; I never heard of the book, and I suspect that most of my teachers never heard of it either. It was not until the late 1960s, with the beginnings of the women's movement, that I discovered that book, and as much as any book can change a life, that book changed mine. What it taught me was that if we try to understand the past and leave women out, we have learned only a partial history, we have a distorted and inadequate sense of the past.

Mary Beard spent forty years of her life writing, speaking, teaching, describing what she called "Woman in Long History." Like her Quaker ancestors, she, too, had a calling, a mission, and it was to reach every person, male and female, to persuade each man and woman of the power and validity of her message. And her message was that women have not only been an oppressed and subject group throughout history, but also active, engaged, productive members of their societies throughout all of time. Women and men have traditionally done different kinds of work in each society, she said, although the kind of work differs from place to place and over time, but the work that men do has virtually always been viewed as more important, more valuable, more brilliant, more creative, more useful, than the work women do and have done. Women are left out of history, I learned from Mary Beard, not because the men—and the few women—who wrote history were bad people, but because these people who wrote the books, who created and shaped the collective wisdom of their societies, focused their attention on those areas of the community in which men predominated and so they actually never saw half the human race.

Mary Beard, through her work and through my reconstruction of her personal life, offered me herself as my mentor, as my model, in a world in which I found no others. She provided me with an intellectual, political, personal, and philosophical sense of woman's place in the world's story. My own small, private existence suddenly had a reality because it was part of a past, a woman's past, a past not alone of struggle and oppression and victimization, but a past of strength and courage and value.

It is not entirely inappropriate to begin a consideration of women's history with a personal account, for that is partly the way Women's Studies evolved, from a personal longing to find oneself, to locate oneself, in the world's story.

The Emergence of Women's History

In 1959 the respected historian David Potter delivered a lecture entitled "American Women and American Character," which he began with an old riddle of two Indians sitting on a fence, one big and one little. The little Indian was the big Indian's son, but the big Indian was not the little Indian's father. How was this possible?

In those days—perhaps even now—we did not think the answer to be that the big Indian is the mother. Indian is perceived as a male category, as opposed to squaw. Sitting on a fence we think of as male activity. If we had said two Indians were mending a tepee or roasting corn, we would have thought about women. In addition, social generalizations are generally thought of in masculine terms. If we had said the little Indian was the daughter, but the big Indian was not the mother, we would more easily have identified the other parent as the father.

The question Potter raised had to do with such unthought-out male bias and how it might influence our way of looking at the past. Are Americans competitive and individualistic, as we often say, or is it American men who are?

Let us take the Frontier thesis of Frederick Jackson Turner, turn-of-the-century U.S. historian, who said that the frontier, created by economic opportunity in the form of free land, influenced the shaping of American character, making Americans individualistic, egalitarian, and independent. Free land for those who could master it. Gold Rush for those who could prospect it. But, Potter pointed out, these were essentially male opportunities. The Cattle Kingdom was a man's world. Mining was a man's world. Women shared in that world, but they had a very different experience, as we learn increasingly every day, and seldom a positive experience. A great deal of feminist scholarship in recent years has confirmed many of David Potter's speculations.

Perhaps the growth of cities was a woman's frontier. The growth of office work, the tending of office machines, perhaps provided avenues for American women to begin to forge their road to autonomy and independence. A woman's symbol may be more appropriately a typewriter rather than a homestead (indeed the operators of the machines were originally called "typewriters"), initially a road to independence and then a shackle from which it is hard for women to free themselves.

These were provocative questions Potter raised in 1959. He was not the first, but he was among the few men to address such concerns. But his ideas, and those of others, were ignored for a good many years. With the women's movement in the late 1960s, launched with Betty Friedan's book *The Feminine Mystique*, came a new look by academics and intellectuals, primarily but not exclusively women, a new look at women's pasts.

The question ultimately took the form of: How would the contours of history be altered if the perspective of women was placed in the center?

When I began teaching courses dealing with Women in History many years ago, people asked, students and colleagues, "Is there such a thing?" How is woman's history different from history, man's history? Certainly there is not women's history apart from men's history. But history as traditionally interpreted has been concerned with activities in which men predominate. Women's History, as it is known, can be thought of as an angle of vision that focuses on the role, perceptions, and behavior of women in the past. Women are not a subgroup, let us remember; we are half of humankind. Still, the focus on women should not diminish the context of history as being a process in which all people are engaged. But so long as we deal heavily with military and political concerns, which is where men have

61

been, and minimize the significance of child-rearing and community-building, for example, we do not see where women have been. It is extraordinary, as Freud said, how we see that which we are trained to see. Women's history tried to make us see differently, to open our historical imaginations, to enable us to challenge the old ways of seeing and thinking.

In reality, if not in the history books, women have always shared equally in the building and shaping of their societies, although differently from men. A sexual division of labor exists in every known society. It is the most basic division in the human story. Women have always worked, as have men, but we have generally worked differently, done different work, and that different work has almost always been valued less than men's work. The sense of the past, then, has come down to us stressing the work and role and activities that were deemed of greater value and impact, the work that men did.

So the first wave of feminist struggle was to compensate for that long period of neglect by locating women who had been left out, primarily women who, by traditional standards, should have been included in our re-creation of the past, women who did much what men did but were not sufficiently noticed.

Then historians of women began to look around more sweepingly to explore social movements that were underrepresented in historical literature. Feminist scholars began to take a new look at the abolitionist movement, the suffrage movement, and religious movements. We always suspected that women did much of the basic work in many organizations, but recent research has indicated that women did more than that. They often initiated activities and shaped policies, but when the organization took root, when more formal structures were required, then men moved into positions of leadership, and they began to keep records. It is the records of men's achievements we have been primarily using. These were movements and activities whose importance was understood, but the place of women in them was unacknowledged.

Only recently, in the past few years, have we come again, because we have been there before, to recognize something else, something different. Many men and women share a common past; however, in profound ways women's historical experience has been different from men's historical experience. It is no less valuable or important, for all its difference. But to try to grasp the dimensions of that experience in a world that has been man-centered, where woman has been the other, the person on the margin, requires an extraordinary stretching of our minds and opening of ourselves to exploring new things and old things in new ways. It is woman-centeredness, and it is hard to envision.

Questioning the Values in the Liberal Arts Curriculum

Let us look at this woman-centeredness in the context of the liberal arts education to which we are all committed. Let us look at the nature and origin of this education, rooted, by and large, in what we call the overriding values of Western civilization.

The values of Western civilization are rooted in assumptions about the collective enterprise we call history that effectively eliminated women. Those who built the foundation of our liberal arts education, those men of the past, were highly privileged products of a very hierarchical society. The idea of a public culture, a set of values that identify an entire civilization, evolved during the Renaissance, and it was during that period that the accepted ideas of Western civilization grew. The emergence of that high public culture evolved to the present, where it is accepted today by many as the only standard of culture, the only method by which one can judge an educated person. The Greeks and Romans, the scholars of the medieval and renaissance universities, were the creators of the tradition we honor and pass on to our students.

The original purpose of that education was to develop the public man, the free and noble man, to create the educated and virtuous gentleman who would participate in and affect the life of the community.

These free and noble people were always and only men. The women we describe as being free and noble were only free compared with other women, not compared with men; that is, they had no access to the public realm, to the seats of learning, to the places of power and decision-making and public influence. Most men were denied access to this realm, but *all* women were. It is the books men wrote, the ideas they developed, and the philosophies they created that are their legacy; and it is to those that we should turn our attention.

Let us look closely at what we have been taught to accept without examination. That is what Women's Studies does, and that is why feminist scholars are not always popular. Since the early 1970s there has been an extraordinary outpouring of scholarship that cries out for a new way of looking at material. The collective body of feminist scholarship has as its goal a transformation of the traditional way of thinking and teaching about history, philosophy, literature, anthropology, biology, even mathematics and physics. Like all new and potentially revolutionary ideas, it is not enthusiastically welcomed into the corridors of learning, for such new ideas are seen as threatening and frightening. They threaten to cause change, and so those who fear change either ignore those ideas or mock them by calling them foolish, unproven, and irrelevant.

The liberal arts education has characterized Western civilization and its values, this high public culture that became the yardstick by which to measure all, as rooted in the assumption that we all belong to a coherent group with shared experiences and similar values. Such a notion can apply to a small group, but such a set of values excludes the diversity that encompasses us all. The cultured gentleman became the standard by which we are all judged, but it is not an appropriate measure of us all.

Are women included in the word mankind? Clearly *no*. When the great philosophers speak of man, they mean man, not human. If you read Aristotle, Kant, Augustine, Rousseau, Marx, Freud, when they write about women, it is clear that they are thinking of women as quite different from men and inferior to men.

Do we not have the right to question the validity of these theories of these great men concerning knowledge, justice, rationality, and politics as we learn that their ideas are rooted in thought that omits half the human race and does not even seem to be aware of it? The answer is that the education we receive is, can only be, partial. To make education whole, to enrich and deepen it, Women's Studies, the placing of women's voice in history and society, is not simply a matter of adding to the pot

64

and stirring, taking an ingredient left out and adding a dash, finding the women who were left out and putting them in. We mean to transform the nature of critical inquiry; we mean to transform the curriculum; we mean to alter profoundly the way we learn and the way we teach. The world will appear to be and will in fact be a different place as the category women becomes a category of analysis to be used in understanding the social order.

We now know that we cannot accept uncritically the traditions that define what is important because those traditions, although they claim universality, in reality deny us. Those traditions need not be rejected, but they must be enlarged, incorporated into new and larger ones. If women are to live within a context, with a sense of location, we need to know about the lives of all our forbears, including our mothers and grandmothers as well as our forefathers. The knowledge and experience of the women who lived before us and to whom we are vitally connected has often been demeaned as trivial, not valuable, not good enough to warrant exploration. Some of their voices are really gone forever, but others can be recovered. For how are we to know ourselves at all, how are we to be educated, truly educated, if we cannot hear their voices?

Reclaiming Women's Past

It is fascinating how the more we look, the more we find. And we do find paintings and sculptures and poetry and stories and weavings and even philosophy created by women, ignored in their time, but good, some excellent, by the prevailing standards of their day.

But most important we are also looking at what women have always done to see if there is greatness there. This is not the traditional greatness we have been taught to believe is the only greatness. We hang quilts on the wall of a museum and only then discover that they are glorious works of art. We hear the song of a Navajo mother singing to her baby, but we do not hear it as serious music unless someone in authority tells us that it is beautiful music. Some musicologists are asking again what it is in some music that makes it great, or that makes us call it great. And what in the folk and women's and black tradition lacks greatness? What makes one inferior to the other?

Once we realize that our notions of what is beautiful and important are too narrow, we are in a new place. We begin to think anew, to admit that we do not yet know; and then we can begin to understand a whole new range of human possibilities.

If women had been present in the creation of the university curriculum, we would know as much of Mary Wollstonecraft, Elizabeth Cady Stanton, Jane Addams, Virginia Woolf, Adrienne Rich, and Sylvia Plath as we do of all the men we study. We would know not only about politics, industry, and war; we would know how a society rears and educates its young and how it builds its local communities. We would know about women's work and its contribution to our civilization. We would be free to think that perhaps the first tool was a hoe or a sling for a baby, as one anthropologist put it, and not necessarily a weapon.

We want to place women in history so that all our humanity can be enlarged, for men, too, need to know about women's pasts. We are reclaiming our reality; we are seeking, if not the whole truth, then more of it than has been available to us until now.

Although there is much to be gained from understanding the cultured gentleman's sense of what is virtuous and good, we cannot be limited by that tradition. That sense of what is proper leaves many of us out, although it tries to argue that we all belong in that tradition. But it is not a set of values that can apply to all of us. We need to have as options many various models, many diverse realities. We must break with the very idea that there is a universal culture that can include us all.

The official texts tell us that women have been only op-pressed and silenced and denied. But while men were doing all the things we know men were doing—creating institutions and ideologies—women were doing something just as important, and we need to know what that was. The theories of the great men do not provide us with the tools or the knowledge to understand the central roles that women have played in the life of the community throughout time.

If we look with care we discover female cultures embedded, almost invisibly, in traditional places. The ever-growing body of feminist scholarship provides us with a new and creative chance to alter, expand, and refine the basic premises on which we build our ideas of the world. Placing women in the historical record, acknowledging the reality of women's true place, permits us to understand more fully the ways in which men and women of different classes and races have shaped the world that we inhabit together.

The domain of public power is the historic sphere of men. The texts with which we are familiar hold and record this collective memory. The world women have traditionally inhabited is a private world of domesticity and reproduction, and that world has little collective memory that is easily accessible to us. But without a knowledge of our own history we live estranged from our own experience. The education we have received until now has not adequately reflected our power or our voice.

The enormous body of feminist scholarship that began about 1970 is so overwhelming in sheer quantity that it is only possible to hint at the range and quality of work being done. No single ideology and no single yardstick has dominated this work. If there is any common theme it is that scholars are impressed with the complexities of women's various experiences. Feminist scholars agree that we must continue to strive for the goal articulated by historian Joan Kelly, of making gender as fundamental to our analysis of the social order as other classifications, such as class and race, but we also realize that we do not even agree on a measure of what constitutes women's status or progress. We need to rethink the very notions of progress and regress. Those who explore that status of women always remind themselves that unlike other subordinate groups, women in general live intimately with their opposites and ordinarily derive their status from their fathers and husbands. Thus it is essential to be aware of the differing situations of women in different classes, castes, and races over time.

New Ways of Finding Women's Past

There is no opportunity in this chapter to explore the different kinds of categories of feminist scholarship except to note that the body of work can be loosely placed in five general categories: work, reproduction, family, sexuality, and ideology.

One of the major contributions offered by the new scholarship on women is the recognition of the validity of studying the private sphere of life and culture and its connection to the public sphere, that is, the acknowledgment of the central place of social relations in an understanding of history.

The entire arena of reproduction, hardly a subject for legitimate and proper research until recently, is now accepted as important. Scholars now recognize the significance and centrality of issues connected with control over pregnancy, abortion, sterilization, and human sexuality in general as social inquiries that address the deepest layers of human experience. Books on the history of birth control, for example, examine that issue within the dimensions of class, politics, and ideology. Those concerns raise further questions about what it means to be a man or a woman, about who determines reproduction and why and how, and about the ideological context in which beliefs about sexual pleasure or their absence are located.

We now recognize the significance for the woman's life process of data concerning the age at which a woman marries, her options, number of children, and life expectancy. We know that the ability of women to control their own fertility is a central fact of women's history, and it has always been carried out one way or another.

Simple demographic information can describe much about the lives of women. In the colonial world, when fertility was high, women spent most of their lives bearing and rearing children. For Quaker women born before 1786, childbearing lasted for 17.4 years, the median age of the mother at birth of the last child was 38 and she survived her last child's departure from home by 4 years. Women born in the 1880s bore children for 11.3 years and lived 20 years after the marriage of the youngest child. In the period from 1950 to 1975 childbearing was over for women at age 30, and the mother was expected to live to age 75. These are important pieces of information for historians in reconstructing the past lives of women.

The institution of motherhood and "mothering-fathering" is new as a subject of historical inquiry. Books by Nancy

Chodorow and Dorothy Dinnerstein address the questions of how girls learn to be mothers and boys learn to be fathers, what the implications are for human relationships, and how psychoanalytic dynamics intersect within the family and cultural context. A study by moral philosopher and psychologist Carol Gilligan suggests that males and females understand aspects of moral decisions in profoundly different ways. We are asking many profound questions for which there currently are no answers.

The history of women comes to us distorted because it comes refracted through the perception of men's observations, through values that define man as the measure, woman as the other. We know that women have always made history as much as men have, but we do not yet know how. But now women are claiming their past and their right to know their past, and they are developing the tools by which to interpret it. To paraphrase the title of a recent book by Gerda Lerner, we are a majority finding its past, for women's history is the history of the majority of humankind. The central notion of women's history is that acknowledging the centrality of women's experience widens the entire base of our understanding of the past and present to encompass the wholeness of life.

Works Cited

Beard, Mary Ritter. *Woman as Force in History.* New York: Macmillan, 1946.

Chodorow, Nancy. *The Reproduction of Mothering.* Berkeley: University of California Press, 1978.

Dinnerstein, Dorothy. *The Mermaid and the Minotaur: Sexual Arrangements and Human Malaise.* New York: Harper & Row, 1976.

Friedan, Betty. *The Feminine Mystique.* New York: Dell, 1963.

Gilligan, Carol. *In a Different Voice.* Cambridge, MA: Harvard University Press, 1982.

Kelly, Joan. *Women, History, and Theory: The Essays of Joan Kelly.* Chicago: University of Chicago Press, 1986.

Lerner, Gerda. *The Creation of Patriarchy.* New York: Oxford University Press, 1986.

CHAPTER 4

Women Artists, Past and Present

ANN SUTHERLAND HARRIS

The History of Professional Women Artists: An Overview

PROFESSIONAL WOMEN ARTISTS have a long history, longer than professional women in any other field. It begins with Greek and Roman legends and can be documented from the tenth century onward, when European women are recorded as producers of embroidered church vestments and illuminated manuscripts. References to women artists are rare, however, and surviving works even rarer until the mid-sixteenth century, when their recorded history begins in earnest with signed and dated works of 1548 by Catherina van Hemessen in Flanders and of 1554 by Sofonisba Anguissola in Italy. They precede by at least a century the emergence of women as professional writers or their tentative entry into the learned professions, from which women were vigorously excluded until this century. The seventeenth-century Englishwoman Aphra Behn was the first to earn her living exclusively from her writings; the first university degree earned by a woman was awarded to Elena Lucrezia Cornaro Piscopia by the University of Padua in 1678.

The number of women artists in Europe and America has grown from a handful of recorded names in the sixteenth century to hundreds of thousands today. For several generations in the United States more women than men have enrolled in art schools and been granted B.F.A. degrees, and 38 percent of all practicing artists in the United States today are women, according to the 1980 census. Whereas women used to be denied a proper training in workshops and academies (the predecessors of the art schools and university art departments that train the majority of artists today), women, by and large, are not unfairly denied admissions or financial support today. But have patriarchal attitudes totally disappeared? How different is the life of a serious, ambitious woman artist today than that of her predecessors? Is a good woman artist as likely as a man to get commissions, sales, exhibitions, and supportive critical response? Do the major museums and most influential art dealers show women as prominently as their numbers would suggest they deserve?

A proper discussion of changing social and political conditions and their effects on artists, male and female, over the past four hundred years, would far exceed the limits of this essay (Harris and Nochlin; Greer; Rubinstein; Munro). Nevertheless, some idea of these changes and artists' responses to them can be grasped by considering three kinds of women painters, past and present, and the degree to which their situations have altered. I will discuss two portrait painters, two still-life painters, and three women artists who painted "mainstream" subjects. The situation of women sculptors is very different; their entry into the profession has been much slower and more recent than that of painters.[1] The situation of women architects and printmakers raises still other issues. These are subjects that still await serious study. This minisurvey can serve as an introduction to the subject of women painters. Luckily, there is now far more good literature in English for those who wish to learn more than was available ten years ago. A more substantial background essay on the history of women artists appears in my introduction to the exhibition catalog *Women Artists, 1550–1950*.

In the sixteenth, seventeenth, and eighteenth centuries, when women could not receive a proper artistic training, those women who became artists tended to be, not surprisingly, the daughters of painters who could study with their fathers. Because women had little or no access to proper study of the human figure (drawing from live nude male models and observing anatomical dissections were thought to be inappropriate activities for a lady), women artists did not usually try to paint the complex, historical compositions which the most ambitious male painters produced in order to win prizes at the salons and success with patrons. Instead women tended to specialize in still life and portraiture (there was no prohibition on studying the clothed human model). Before the middle of the nineteenth century, only an exceptionally courageous and talented woman would try to become a "history painter," and she would face almost insurmountable obstacles in order to do so. No such barriers exist today, only the financial barriers posed by exceptionally expensive material (the cost of casting a plaster sculpture model in steel, for example). Patrons are still more inclined to support a man who applies for funds to create a large piece of sculpture than a woman, but even the special financial barriers posed by ambitious sculptural commissions have been cracked by women in the last generation. Although not as ubiquitous in public sites as the bronze shapes of Henry Moore, the intricate walls of Louise Nevelson have been installed in many corporate collections as well as in most major museums in America, and a group of younger women sculptors including Beverly Pepper, Lila Katzen, Linda Howard, Alice Aycock, and Mary Miss have been awarded major public commissions for bronzes and site installations.

Portraiture: Elisabeth Vigée-Lebrun and Alice Neel

Elisabeth Vigée-Lebrun (1755–1842) and Alice Neel (1900–84) both painted portraits for most of their careers and are associated with this genre of painting more than with any other, yet both resisted being categorized as portrait painters. Both women were well aware of the dubious status of their chosen specialty. Theorists argued that to copy one figure from life was a far less demanding task than creating many types and poses from the imagination and arranging them in an effective composition. To demonstrate her capacity to be more than a portraitist, Vigée-Lebrun painted an allegorical composition with two women figures as her *pièce de réception* when she joined the Royal Academy in Paris in 1783, thus earning her the more prestigious rank of history painter. However, almost all her paintings are portraits, although a few contain more than one figure. She was enormously successful. She had received her first royal commission when she was twenty, and had painted Queen Marie Antoinette and many of the most powerful aristocrats in her circle before the French Revolution. Then Vigée's close connections with the court became a dangerous handicap. She and her young daughter escaped to Rome, and the artist spent the next twenty years in exile, traveling from Italy to Austria, Poland, Russia, and England, painting her masterful and exceedingly flattering portraits of aristocratic men, women, and children everywhere she went. She was one of the great celebrities of her day (Baillio).

Alice Neel would not have liked Elisabeth Vigée-Lebrun. Although both women had their unconventional sides, Neel was, even for the 1920s, a woman of ferocious independence who had led her life as she wished and not as society thought she and other women should (Hill). She was born outside Philadelphia in 1900 and finished her training at the Moore College of Art (then the Philadelphia College of Design) in 1924. After the failure of her first marriage to a Cuban painter, the death of her first child from diphtheria, and the loss of her second child (who at fourteen was taken to Cuba by the father), Neel had a breakdown. Her desire to draw and paint saved her, and she slowly built up her life again and had two sons by two different men, neither of whom she married. She lived alone on a very modest income (the Works Progress Administration kept her alive during the Depression and for many years afterward), painting pictures of people who interested her, not people who wanted Neel to paint them. Neel thus reversed the usual relationship between sitter and artist; by doing so she freed herself to paint people as she saw them, not as they wanted to be seen.

Vigée's success depended on her ability to flatter her sitters and make them look slightly more elegant, poised, and cultivated than they were. Neel despised such an approach as compromising her artistic integrity. She was not interested in the surface and in polite conventions. She wanted to reveal the inner personalities of her subjects with all their tensions, ambiguities, and force. She also wanted to paint a portrait of her times, a human panorama of types and psyches, and if the sitter could not afford to buy the result or disliked it, Neel did not care. She was unwavering in her artistic goal, even when the mainstream decreed that the only serious art was abstract, and no one exhibited her work, reviewed it, or bought it.

Neel only began to have some real recognition and some modest financial success in the 1960s, in part because Pop Art made human imagery of an unconventional kind respectable again. She painted Andy Warhol and a number of other artists and celebrities, had a modest retrospective at the Whitney Museum in 1974, and showed regularly with an established Madison Avenue dealer. Until the end, however, many viewers and critics could not forgive Neel for her insistence on seeing people her way and delving behind their emotional defenses to find the vulnerable human being within. She was accused of reducing her sitters to caricatures and of waging psychological warfare against them.

Male artists such as Warhol, Philip Pearlstein, Alex Katz, and Chuck Close, whose interpretations of the portrait have had far greater success with critics and collectors than Neel's, have in common a cool, formalistic emphasis that allows little of the sitter's psyche to penetrate the picture plane. This emotional distancing fits the stereotype of the male as controlled and rational, while Neel's more exposed psychological content answers to the opposite stereotype of the woman as a moody creature subject to temperamental fits and, of course, partly explains why her paintings are taken far less seriously and fetch lower prices than Warhol's mass-produced, silk-screened celebrity images or Katz's bland billboard figures. Neel's work demands far more of the viewer than does the work of her male counterparts. In effect, she asks you what you feel about this pregnant woman, or an old man dying of cancer, or a poor black woman with a mortally ill child, or a black man who has had a lung collapsed because of tuberculosis, or an unhappy heterosexual couple, or a happy gay couple, or a schizophrenic, or a thief, or an old socialist, or a young intellectual. Her own intense engagement with each human being she has painted glows from each canvas. There is no way that the human content can be ignored or the painting discussed only in terms of its formal structure.

If we juxtapose one of Elisabeth Vigée-Lebrun's rare depictions of a female nude with one of Alice Neel's nude portraits, the differences in the social and professional situations of both women are sharply emphasized. Vigée painted an occasional nude primarily to establish, however tenuously, her claim to be a serious painter who had fully mastered the human figure, despite the Royal Academy's prohibition of women students at life-drawing sessions, and thus to claim her place among other French eighteenth-century painters of the female figure, such as Nattier, Fragonard, and Boucher. Her *Bacchante* (1785, Musée Nissim Camondo, Paris) shows a coy, beautiful woman posing so as to suggest that she is slightly tipsy and available. Alice Neel's *Margaret Evans Pregnant,* with its down-to-earth approach to sex and nudity, comments on the artificiality of Vigée's woman. Pregnancy fascinated Neel, in part because she liked to paint people under stress, and the final stages of pregnancy are a strain. In the last trimester a pregnant woman cannot bend over because of the precious, growing lump in her middle that increasingly makes eating, excreting, sleeping, and even breathing difficult. You can search art history for any portrayals of nude, pregnant women before Neel, let alone one of such honesty, and, except in photographs, you will find none. Even the photographs celebrate that foggy ideal of woman in tune with nature, the quintessential earth mother, all curves and tenderness, whether or not the photographer is male or female. Neel painted ten or more magnificent nude portraits of pregnant women, some reclining, others seated, and painted one woman in the throes of labor based on memories of the experiences of the woman in the bed beside Neel when she had her third child. As far as I know, all these paintings still belong to members of Neel's own family, this despite the fact that the female nude is normally an irresistible subject.

Another comparison that underlines Vigée's acceptance of the conventions of the society into which she was born and Neel's firm opposition to the status quo is that between one of Vigée's grand, official portraits of Queen Marie Antoinette (1787, Palais de Versailles) and Neel's portrait of Mayor Edward Koch (1981). Neither Koch nor the city of New York commissioned his portrait. The mayor had seen Neel's own nude *Self Portrait,* painted when she was eighty (National Museum of American

75

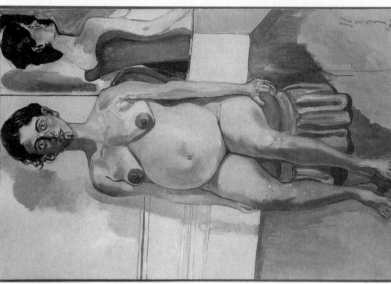

↑ Copy after Elisabeth Vigée-Lebrun:
Bacchante (Bacchante Assise), 1785
By permission of The Fine Arts Museums of San
Francisco, Mildred Anna Williams Collection

Alice Neel: *Margaret Evans Pregnant*, 1978 →
Courtesy the Robert Miller Gallery, New York

"Vigée painted an occasional nude primarily to establish . . . her
claim to be a serious painter who had fully mastered the human
figure. . . . Her *Bacchante* . . . shows a coy, beautiful woman pos–

ing so as to suggest that she is slightly tipsy and available. Alice
Neel's *Margaret Evans Pregnant*, with its down-to-earth approach to
sex and nudity, comments on the artificiality of Vigée's woman."

Art), and when he contacted the artist, she managed, in her inimitable way, to get him to agree to pose for her. Vigée's portrait shows the queen surrounded by her children in a palatial setting conjured up by vistas and marble columns, swags of velvet drapes, silk cords, tassels, and symbols of royalty. Ed Koch is shown in his shirt-sleeves in one of the unpretentious chairs that appears in many other Neel portraits. There are no trappings of office, no cloak or gold chain, not a hint that we are facing one of America's most powerful politicians, although we can detect his astute mind and sharp wit.

Official portraiture is now moribund, if not actually dead. None of America's best-known portraitists paint the President, senators, or chief executive officers for board room settings, and the artists who do supply these images still are nonentities. Neel's unconventional presentation of an important public figure proves, among other things, that she did not really paint portraits, but people she liked, that she was intrigued by, that she believed were representative in some way of the communal psyche of twentieth-century America. It was a very different artistic vision from that of Vigée, who supported the aristocracy and the social order they defined until her death. Vigée provided a flattering, comforting interpretation of the self-image of those she portrayed. Neel did not, nor would she alter her style or artistic intentions to make the work more salable. Vigée defied convention only by being a woman painter. Her art was in no way unconventional, and because she was an exceptionally charming and attractive woman, her path to social success with the patrons she needed was a smooth one. Neel was always a rebel, opinionated, involved in social causes, passionate about everything she did, and utterly uninterested in domestic accomplishments and a lady-like appearance. It is not hard to understand why she received so little support in her lifetime. It is just unfortunate that, unlike Eakins, she did not inherit sufficient private income to live comfortably while pursuing her artistic vision.

Did Neel's sex prevent her from receiving greater recognition? The answer is not easy. Although probably a factor, it is significant that another female figurative painter, Isabel Bishop, who is of the same generation as Neel, has had far more success

Elisabeth Vigée-Lebrun: *Marie Antoinette and Her Children*, 1787
Palais de Versailles; Ets. J. E. Bulloz, Paris

Alice Neel: *Portrait of Mayor Koch*, 1981 →
Courtesy the Robert Miller Gallery, New York

These two portraits of official personages underline "Vigée's acceptance of the conventions of the society into which she was born and
Neel's firm opposition to the status quo." Vigée's portrait was one of
many royal commissions she received. Neel persuaded Koch to sit for
her. Her presentation of him in his shirt-sleeves, with no trappings of
office, "proves, among other things, that she [painted] people she
liked, that she was intrigued by, that she believed were representative
in some way of the communal psyche of twentieth-century America."

in finding patronage and support and is regularly mentioned in histories of American art of the 1930s, 1940s, and 1950s. Bishop is a gracious, lady-like woman, immaculately dressed and very unbohemian. Moreover, her images of men and women shopping, eating in cafeterias, enjoying a break from work in a city park, and so on lack the bitter social comment and intense, psychological probing of Neel's work (Lunde; Harris and Nochlin 360). Bishop's work does not make the viewer faintly uncomfortable, but rather skirts the darker sides of human nature. Their male contemporaries, artists like Yasio Kuniyoshi, Raphael and Moses Soyer, and Ben Shahn, also produced human images that were more conventional, and thus more comfortable, than those of Neel. Yet, in recent years, Neel has received far more critical attention than they have, although this attention has primarily focused on her more recent work. Indeed since the late 1960s, she has had more recognition from collectors, museums, and exhibition curators than she had had during the preceding sixty years. She still did not command the prices or prestigious gallery sponsorship of younger male figure painters, such as Alex Katz, Philip Pearlstein, or Chuck Close, but she became a celebrity among women artists (she was a spectacular speaker, funny, outrageous, and wise in rapid succession) and is gradually making her way into the pantheon of important American artists of this century.

Still-life Painting: Rachel Ruysch and Janet Fish

A quick look at the status of still-life painting in the seventeenth and eighteenth centuries and today, and of women artists associated with that genre, also underlines the enormous change in the situation facing women artists today. The genre only emerges as a popular category of art throughout Europe in the seventeenth century. It was a specialty in which some seventeenth- and eighteenth-century women painters were very successful. The reasons women chose this genre—and they were among its pioneers—again have to do with their exclusion from life-drawing classes and the related training given to male painters.

Portraying bowls of fruit and vases of flowers on a table presented no social difficulties whatsoever. Indeed it encouraged the woman to remain safely at home. The same social conventions made it almost impossible for women to go on sketching trips in the countryside and so prepare to become landscape painters, a genre in which women are almost unknown until the nineteenth century. The compositional formulas popular at the beginning were not demanding—a few objects like shells, fruit, or flowers arranged almost symmetrically and parallel to the picture plane. What patrons wanted was a fine illusion of reality, and maybe a commonplace allusion of mortality (a butterfly, a full-blown tulip). The genre still exists today as a recognizable category of realistic painting, but apart from Giorgio Morandi, no twentieth-century still-life specialist has a substantial reputation. Still, the genre continues to appeal to artists and patrons for some of the reasons that account for its popularity in the nineteenth century. The ability to paint an illusion of reality never ceases to fascinate, even after a hundred years of photography, and images of satisfyingly arranged domestic possessions, or species of fruit and flowers, appeal to a universal need for images of order and perfection to contemplate amid the chaos and imperfections of daily life.

The finest woman still-life painter of the seventeenth- andeighteenth centuries probably was Rachel Ruysch of Amsterdam, although some would argue that the Parisians Louise Moillon (1610–96) and Anna Vallayer-Coster (1744–1818) are her equal (Harris and Nochlin). Ruysch perfected rather than invented the flower piece, and she was a spectacular exponent of these images of horticultural perfection. Born in 1664, the daughter of a botanist and the granddaughter of an important architect, Ruysch came from a supportive intellectual and artistic household and was painting professionally in her late teens. Unlike Moillon, she continued to paint despite marriage to another artist and the birth of ten children, and was active even in her eighties, although her eyesight had deteriorated by then; her best works were made between 1690 and 1730. Her paintings displayed considerable knowledge of botany and entomology as well as sophisticated coloring, compositional orchestration, and virtuoso illusionism. She was very successful during her lifetime, and collectors ever since have ensured that top prices are paid for her finest pieces.

One contemporary woman also enjoys a considerable reputation for still-life painting—Janet Fish (1938–   ), who is best known for large oil paintings of transparent bottles, goblets, empty jelly glasses, or other shiny objects grouped together and rendered with vigorous realism. Although the illusion of the groupings of bottles and glasses is impressive, perhaps even more so is the artist's ability to achieve her effects without resorting to a technique of meticulous precision. Recent works have included figures, such as one of a young woman asleep on a kitchen table beside a spilled bag of groceries and household products, a modern allegory of sloth recalling those made by Dutch painters in the seventeenth century, except that now one senses the artist's sympathy with any woman facing those daily, repetitive, unrewarding chores rather than the challenge of artistic creation (Rubinstein 379, 392–94).[2] Fish is a successful painter whose work is handled by a major New York dealer, and she is certainly one of a handful of artists now painting still life who receive serious critical support as well as the satisfaction of selling their work.

"Mainstream" Subjects: Artemisia Gentileschi, Miriam Schapiro, and Joyce Kozloff

The real test of women's successful integration into the contemporary art world is their status in the most prestigious categories, such as large sculpture commissions and works, in whatever medium, in the styles currently thought to be the most exciting. The situation facing any artist today is infinitely more complex than it was even a hundred years ago, when the official salon system began to disintegrate. Status and anti-status are not so easily defined. No sooner has Soho become *the* place for a successful Manhattan dealer in contemporary art to have his or her gallery than Tribeca and the East Village become the darlings of the critics. Sculpture is no longer made of bronze or marble by those seeking success, but may be made of steel, discarded lumber, wrecked cars, canvas stuffed with kapok, polyurethane, fiberglass, roofing tiles, or mesquite wood carved with a chain saw (this last medium used by a young woman sculptor from Texas, who certainly had her tongue in her cheek as she buzzed away), to name only a small sampling of the incredibly varied materials used in recent work *(Art in America)*.[3] The boundary lines between painting and sculpturing are also impossible to draw as painters make sculpture or wall reliefs and sculptors paint their works and prop them against the wall. The critics and the public, scorched so often in the past for condemning the avant-garde, seem willing to accept anything that is not obviously derivative or meekly incompetent.

Not only are there no rules anymore about what is and is not art, but there have never been so many gifted artists trying to make a living in America. The result is a horrendously competitive atmosphere caused by thousands of gifted artists of all ages struggling to catch the attention of the few critics, collectors, and curators in every major American city. Add to this situation the dearth of serious intelligible critical writing outside New York and Los Angeles (and not much in those cities either), and the dearth of serious, independent (as opposed to sheep-like trend) collecting everywhere, and you will have some understanding of the mixture of chutzpah, luck, and talent that a good artist needs today to survive, let alone be a success. As mentioned earlier, 38 percent of the artists in America today are women. There is, however, no major museum or department of contemporary art with a permanent collection of which 38 percent is by women artists, nor do any of these museums or departments devote 38 percent of their one-person exhibitions to women artists. With a few exceptions, 5 percent would be a generous estimate of the percentage of their resources devoted to the achievements of women artists. Sometimes it seems as if little has changed since 1772, when the French Royal Academy declared that it would only accept four women members. The quota permitted today is an unspoken one, but it is a fact of life that a very small percentage of women artists make it to the blue-chip realm of steady support by a major Manhattan dealer, annual or biannual shows that are sold out even before the opening, works on permanent exhibit in the contemporary galleries of major museums, patrons queuing up for works as they are completed, and incomes well into six figures. Although it is true that many fine male artists also live on the edge of starvation, census figures on incomes show that women artists, on average, earn a third of what male artists do, far less than the sixty-one cents that all working women earn compared with every dollar earned by the average working man.

This is not the place to analyze discrimination against contemporary women artists in detail, although it should be obvious that when a substantial element involved in judging achievement is subjective, as is the case with all the arts, it is easier for discrimination to persist. If a woman in the business world launches a new product and it makes a million dollars for her company, it would be shortsighted to deny her a promotion. If a woman artist creates a masterpiece that only one critic notices in print because the others are busy writing mainly about male artists, whom they instinctively believe are more likely to be making important art, she may well die unrecognized, or end her career prematurely because she has received so little encouragement, or produce poorer work because she has trouble believing in her creative ability in the face of critical silence. All this background is necessary if one is to appreciate the different kinds of achievement in a hostile environment represented by the work of Artemisia Gentileschi in seventeenth-century Rome and Miriam Schapiro and Joyce Kozloff in twentieth-century New York.

Artemisia Gentileschi, who was born in Rome in 1593 and died in Naples about sixty years later, was the first woman painter who affected the style of other (that is, male) artists (Harris and Nochlin 118–24; Bissell 153).[4] Her father, Orazio, who was eight years older than Michelangelo da Caravaggio, had begun a career as a rather conventional fresco painter in Rome when Caravaggio arrived from Milan and began painting his astonishingly naturalistic pictures of young men holding baskets of fruit. Orazio became his most sensitive Italian follower. He did not, however, omit settings for his stories, as Caravaggio often did, nor the fresco medium, which Caravaggio never used, and he preferred a more varied palette than the red, yellow, black, brown, and white characteristic of Caravaggio's mature work. The result is a more lyrical interpretation of Caravaggio's naturalism, which may be less profound but is in its own way more beautiful.

Artemisia had the advantage, therefore, not only of living in the artistic capital of Europe, but also of growing up in the household of a very good painter, who could teach her the fundamentals of her craft from her childhood. Orazio also hired other artists to teach her what he could not—perspective. A man he hired to do this, Agostino Tassi, seduced Artemisia, was sued by her father for rape, and imprisoned (in 1611–12). Artemisia was married off to an older man and moved to Florence, away from the scandal in Rome, shortly after the trial ended. There she painted and exhibited her infamous *Judith Decapitating Holofernes* (Uffizi Gallery). Men have painted this subject many times without their personal lives being mentioned when the painting is discussed, but Artemisia's unhappy experiences with Tassi are always cited as background to the Uffizi picture, and probably with reason. However, she chose the subject not merely to enact a vicarious visual revenge on the deceitful Tassi, who had promised to marry her and had stolen works by her father. She was also ambitious to prove herself the equal of her male contemporaries, for its composition is a clever critique of Caravaggio's earlier depiction of the same story. Caravaggio's Judith executes her task in a sort of languid haze that does not promise success without divine intervention. Artemisia's Judith tackles the unpleasant deed with the down-to-earth determination of Julia Child demonstrating how to carve a turkey (Hibbard 66; *The Age of Caravaggio* 258).

At the age of seventeen, before she left Rome, Artemisia painted an ambitious picture of Susanna spied on by the elders that is now in a private German collection. No less astonishing than its sophisticated composition, subtle drawing, and psychological awareness is Artemisia's choice of history subjects involving full-scale figures, even nudes, at the beginning of her career. She was clearly determined to escape from the safe niche of portraits and still lifes and challenge male artists in the one area they tacitly believed women could not enter, that of full-scale religious, mythological, and historical narrative paintings for public and private patrons.

Artemisia Gentileschi: *Judith Decapitating Holofernes*, 1615/20
Pitti; Alinari/Art Resource, NY; cf. Judith 13:1–13

Artemisia chose subjects "to prove herself the equal of her male contemporaries, for its composition [Judith] is a clever critique of Caravaggio's earlier depiction of the same story. Caravaggio's Judith executes her task in a sort of languid haze that does not promise success. . . . Artemisia's Judith tackles the unpleasant deed with down-to-earth determination. . . . At the age of seventeen . . . Artemisia painted an ambitious picture of Susanna spied on by the elders. . . . No less astonishing than its sophisticated composition . . . is Artemisia's choice of history subjects involving full-scale figures, even nudes, at the beginning of her career."

Artemisia Gentileschi: *Susanna and the Elders,* 1610
Pommersfelden, Schloss Weissenstein, Dr. Karl Graf van Schonbrun-
Wiesenheid; Marburg/Art Resource, NY
Cf. *Douay Bible,* Daniel 13:19–27

87

Artemisia did on occasion paint portraits (only two certain examples survive), but her energies were always focused on figure-painting. Because she could not draw from the male nude, she used female models, whom the rules of propriety forbade men to study, and she flaunts her knowledge of the female anatomy in several works by showing the heroines wearing far less than was traditional for those subjects (Bissell). Her letters complain of the expense entailed in finding suitable female models and also insist that her patrons pay her the same fee given to her male competitors. She comes across in the letters, as in her works, as a woman of great determination, ambition, and character who fully succeeded in her aim to become a serious painter by the standards of her day.

However, she did not have as much success as women artists who specialized in portraiture and still life. She was not as famous as Sofonisba Anguissola, whose reputation came in part from being the first Italian woman artist to be patronized by popes and kings (Harris and Nochlin 106). Nor was she a celebrity like Rosalba Carriera (1675–1757), whose flattering pastel portraits were sought by English and French visitors to Venice. Undoubtedly these women were tolerated more readily by their male peers because they were not competing with them for the most prestigious kinds of commissions (indeed, with one exception that may be only legend, no woman in the fourteenth to eighteenth century became a fresco painter, long considered the most challenging and difficult kind of painting in Italy). Carriera created her own market by essentially inventing the pastel head-and-shoulders portrait, and the foreigners who came to Venice on the Grand Tour, in part to have themselves portrayed by her, also bought views of Venice and mythologies by other painters to decorate their palaces and country houses. Giulia Lama (c. 1683–1753), who tried to paint public altarpieces in Venice while Carriera was painting portraits, was ostracized by her male peers and received few commissions (Harris and Nochlin 16ff., 165ff.). The message clearly was that a few women artists could be tolerated in their place, but that the most important and prestigious kinds of art could only be made by men.

What kind of a reception does a woman artist receive today if she participates in a movement that receives extensive critical attention? The answer is mixed. The major movements of the twentieth century since Impressionism (Post-Impressionism, Cubism, Surrealism, Expressionism, Constructivism, Abstraction Expressiónism, Pop, Op, Minimalism, Conceptual Art, Photorealism, Neo-Expressionism, to name only some) have all had important women participants, but in most cases we have had to wait for recent publications by younger scholars open to the theories of feminism to do justice to their contributions. Only recently has Lee Krasner's role in the development of Abstract Expressionism been examined and has a full account been given of the vital role of women in the Surrealist movement (Rose, *Krasner/Pollock;* Rose, *Lee Krasner;* Chadwick). Marisol, an important sculptor and painter best known for her Pop constructions of the 1960s, continues to do passionate, beautiful, and technically innovative work, but she no longer gets extensive press coverage. Vasaraley's Op prints and Agam's Op reliefs, which I find boring, are on show in many major museums, while the subtlest manipulator of the optical geometry and color of them all, Edna Andrade, is little known outside Philadelphia, where she lives. Audrey Flack, the only major woman active as a photorealist and one of the inventors of that movement, was extensively criticized for using female cultural icons in her work, while male photorealists were not similarly taken to task for their obsessions with cars and motorcycles (Flack 10, 27).

One recent art movement bears special watching by feminist critics because it was invented by women and then joined by men, almost certainly the first time this has happened in the twentieth century and perhaps in the history of art. Pattern and Decoration was a movement invented by women, specifically Joyce Kozloff and Miriam Schapiro. They set out to challenge the traditional low value accorded to decoration in the arts and to make high art using decorative art that they admired. They and a number of other artists who shared their views had considerable success in the 1970s. However, when the Museum of Modern Art reopened its expanded galleries in 1982 with a survey of the art of the seventies, two *male* Pattern and Decoration painters, Robert Kushner and Robert Zakanich, were included, not women. And so it goes.

A small number of twentieth-century women are admitted to the Pantheon of Superstars, and the rest have to make do with occasional flashes of limelight and silence. (My criteria for superstar status include acquisitions by major museums and collectors, feature articles in national art magazines, inclusion in major contemporary survey shows such as the Whitney Biennial, the Carnegie International, and representation by major New York dealers.) The current female residents of the Western World Art Pantheon (WWAP) are Georgia O'Keeffe, Barbara Hepworth, Louise Nevelson, Helen Frankenthaler, Joan Mitchell, Eva Hesse, and Agnes Martin. Many other women have been contenders and then, as with Marisol, their work is no longer so visible. Among younger women currently on tenure track for future promotion to the WWAP are Jennifer Bartlett, Cindy Sherman, Susan Rothenberg, and Elizabeth Murray. It is particularly strange that none of the large cohort of women sculptors who have emerged with such strength and vitality since the late 1960s should appear to have a secure niche in the tenure track toward eternal fame, but not even Louise Bourgeois has that status, despite a retrospective at the Museum of Modern Art, to judge by the rarity of her work on show in major museums. Younger women, despite being handled by established dealers and commanding substantial prices, are less securely established than men like Donald Judd, Arnaldo Pomodoro, Tony Smith, Robert Smithson, and John Chamberlain. Still, the creative strength displayed by Jackie Winsor, Jackie Ferrara, Mary Miss, Lynda Benglis, Alice Aycock, Beverly Pepper, Harmony Hammond, Nancy Graves, and Barbara Zucker, among others, is so forceful that I doubt they can be eliminated from the history of twentieth-century sculpture. Judy Pfaff even has a color plate of one of her vibrant installations in the revised, new edition of H. W. Janson's *History of Art,* an introductory art history textbook infamous for including no women artists long after the other introductory survey texts had done so.

The future critical fate of Pattern and Decoration should be watched, along with that of the male and female artists involved in it, precisely because this is the first twentieth-century art movement started by women and then joined by men. Will their role be acknowledged by future historians, or will their achievements somehow be subsumed by the work of the men who joined them and used it, as is their right, for their own artistic purposes.

Kozloff (b. 1942) is attracted by Islamic interlace; by ceramic tiles used in Mexican, Hispano-Moresque, Turkish, and Persian architecture; by traditional quilt patterns; and by local American decorative traditions in the cities where she has worked (Johnston et al.). Miriam Schapiro (b. 1923) has made her art out of textiles with female, domestic associations—lace, fringes, sequins, glass beads, embroidery, flowered chintzes, and brocades—which she has collaged together in large compositions based on the shapes of houses, fans, hearts, and kimonos (Gouma-Peterson).[5] Both women are highly knowledgeable about the traditions that they work with and the symbols incorporated into their work. Both women are feminists and both wanted the decorative traditions and crafts that they incorporated into their work to be as highly valued as other art forms.

The men who joined the "P and D movement," as it was quickly dubbed, hide its origins and sources more deliberately than the women, for whom these are essential to the meaning of the work. Both Kozloff, who has received a number of major public commissions to provide tile murals in bus stations, subway stations, and airports, and Schapiro, whose work sells steadily to major collectors, have had considerable critical and financial success, but even they have not attracted the attention of all the most famous male critics; and it is rare to see work by either woman in a major museum. In the case of Kozloff it may be argued that her finest work does not belong there because it is so carefully designed for a particular public site, where in fact it will be seen by many more people and many classes of people than would ever study an installation in a museum. In reaching out to a larger, less sophisticated audience for her art, Kozloff is also challenging the role of the museum as the final arbiter of taste for contemporary art as well as traditional aesthetic values.

She also resembles some of her female predecessors in finding success by creating a new art form that does not directly compete with the male establishment.

Women in the Contemporary Art World

In my experience contemporary women artists are more concerned that their message be understood by their audience than most male artists are. Women are more likely to provide a statement that offers substantial clues to any personal symbolism used, and if the work is intensely autobiographical, as it often is, they never lose sight of the universal behind the particular. One curator who sees a great deal more current art than I do believes that women's work typically has more emotional warmth and resonance than that of male artists, who prefer a more detached, cool stance to their own psyches and those of others. Certainly, if we compare Robert Longo or David Salle with Audrey Flack or May Stevens, the content of the women's work is clearer, more didactic even, but still very personal without being trite or obvious (Flack; Stevens).[6] Salle's statements in interviews, by contrast, are dense and unhelpful, and his imagery, much of which seems to come from hard-core pornography, is blatantly insulting to women. Fear and hatred of women and the boredom of his own existence would seem to be his only message. Flack and Stevens have dealt with many large issues in their work—family relationships, the passage of time, the importance of friendship, personal crises, and tragedies—and found their own visual language to convey their moral concerns. I find their art far more moving and far more aesthetically engaging than that by the male figurative painters currently in vogue (Salle, Longo, Julian Schnabel, Eric Fischl). Mine is, however, only one small critical voice in a large, noisy orchestra, although it may be significant that Salle's work in particular has recently inspired several articulate essays that attack rather than praise it (Fernandez 32–34; Mullarkey 619–28; Danto 302).

There are hundreds of important women artists now active in

WOMEN IN AMERICA EARN ONLY 2/3 OF WHAT MEN DO.
WOMEN ARTISTS EARN ONLY 1/3 OF WHAT MEN ARTISTS DO.

A PUBLIC SERVICE MESSAGE FROM **GUERRILLA GIRLS**, CONSCIENCE OF THE ART WORLD

all media in the United States. If the greatest honors are still given more readily to men than to women, women have nevertheless won a far larger share of attention in the contemporary art world than they have ever had before. The latest phase of the women's movement has had an enormous effect here, as on every other sphere of American cultural, social, and political life. Still, the major institutions will need prodding and pushing for another decade or so from organizations like the Women's Caucus for Art and the Guerrilla Girls, an anonymous group who create and distribute witty posters publicizing the minimal role of women artists in most major museums, major art surveys, and major commercial galleries. The new Museum of Women in the Arts in Washington, which opened in April 1986, should also help by providing an elegant setting for serious exhibitions devoted to many aspects of women's artistic achievements, a growing permanent collection, and research facilities. Slowly, women will assume their rightful position in the visual arts. The more women and men who are aware of women's past and current achievements, the easier it will be.

Notes

1. Louise Nevelson, Eva Hesse, and Jackie Winsor, together with two husband-and-wife teams (the Keinholzes and the Poiriers), were included in the major survey of twentieth-century European sculpture at the Guggenheim Museum in the spring of 1986, an exhibition that included twenty artists.

2. The painting mentioned, *Darlene and the Groceries,* appeared as the illustration for February in the 1987 *Women Painters* Calendar (Abbeville Press).

3. None of the major articles in the March 1987 issue of *Art in America* are on women. *Art News* devotes a higher percentage of its editorial space to women artists and is to be recommended for that reason.

4. An excellent book on Artemisia Gentileschi by Mary Garrard will be published by Princeton University Press in 1988.

5. The work discussed in *Miriam Schapiro: A Retrospective: 1953–1980,* edited and curated by Thalia Gouma-Peterson, is only the most recent phase of a long, complex career embracing Abstract Expressionism and Geometric Abstraction before Schapiro became a feminist and sought to express her beliefs in her art.

6. Stevens' book, *Ordinary, Extraordinary,* explores the artist's concern with the life of her own mother (an ordinary woman) and that of Rosa Luxemburg (an extraordinary woman).

Works Cited

The Age of Caravaggio. New York: Metropolitan Museum of Art, 1985.

Art in America, March 1987.

Baillio, Joseph, ed. *Elisabeth Louise Vigée Le Brun, 1755–1842,* Fort Worth, TX: Kimbell Art Museum, 1982.

Bissell, R. Ward. "Artemisia Gentileschi—A New Documented Chronology." *Art Bulletin* 50 (1968):153f.

Chadwick, Whitney. *Women Artists and the Surrealist Movement.* Boston: NY Graphic Society Books, 1985.

Danto, Arthur C. "Salle's Sullen Art." *The Nation* 7 (1987):302.

Fernandez, Joyce. "Images of Women in the Art of David Salle." *New Art Examiner,* Nov. 1986, 32–34.

Flack, Audrey. *Audrey Flack on Painting.* New York: H. N. Abrams, 1984.

Gouma-Peterson, Thalia, ed. *Miriam Schapiro: A Retrospective: 1953–1980.* Wooster, OH: The College of Wooster, 1980.

Greer, Germaine. *The Obstacle Race*. New York: Farrar, Straus & Giroux, 1979.

Harris, Ann Sutherland, and Linda Nochlin. *Women Artists, 1550–1950*. New York: Alfred Knopf, 1977.

Hibbard, Howard. *Caravaggio*. New York: Harper & Row, 1983.

Hill, Patricia. *Alice Neel*. New York: H. N. Abrams, 1983.

Janson, H. W. *History of Art*. New York: H. N. Abrams, 1986.

Johnston, Patricia, et al. *Joyce Kozloff: Visionary Ornament*. Boston: Boston University Art Gallery, 1986.

Lunde, Karl. *Isabel Bishop*. New York: H. N. Abrams, 1975.

Mullarkey, Maureen. "The Figure and How It Fared." *The Hudson Review* 40 (1987):619–28.

Munro, Eleanor. *Originals: American Women Artists*. New York: H. N. Abrams, 1979.

Rose, Barbara. *Krasner/Pollock: A Working Relationship*. New York: New York University, 1981.

———. *Lee Krasner: A Retrospective*. New York: Museum of Modern Art, 1981.

Rubinstein, Charlotte Streifer. *American Women Artists*. New York: G. K. Hall, 1982.

Stevens, Alice. *Ordinary, Extraordinary*. 1970.

CHAPTER 5

Feminist Film Comes of Age
Recent Works by Women Directors

JULIA REICHERT

As WE LOOK BACK on almost twenty years since the beginning of the "second wave" women's movement and count our victories, one surely is the emergence of films by women. Feminist struggle has brought major changes both on the screen and behind the camera. In the 1980s we have female "buddy" films, black female stars, female heroes in outer space, positive lesbian themes, mother-daughter conflict, adolescent girl's rebellion, interesting older women; in short, dimensional female characters in real stories. We also have women directors, animators, documentarians, writers, cinematographers, sound engineers, and technicians in larger numbers than ever, although still far too few.

But has women's cinema come of age? Not yet! It is only recently out of grade school. Its history is very short, and this is no wonder.

Reflect for a moment. Doesn't it seem strange that with all the thousands of films that have been made up until 1980, only a tiny handful have been directed, produced, photographed, or written by women? Of the major institutions and industries in American society, Hollywood has been one of the most resistant to the feminist challenge. Of the almost 1,000 directing assignments since 1980, only 32 have gone to women. One male producer said, "A woman can handle the family's shopping budget, but don't let her loose on a $5 million feature budget." Others feel that because directors must command the respect of actors and crew, they must be father figures. Women are not taken seriously enough to be directors. "Ms. Treatment," an excellent article in *Film Comment,* chronicles the painful stories of blatant sexism: sexual favors expected in exchange for jobs, discrimination in technical jobs, pats on the head and the be-hind, and psychological harassment. That is the bad news.

But to look only to Hollywood is to miss the major story of women and film in America. Until recently that story is to be found outside Tinseltown, in the independent film community. This community exists in every region of our country and includes women of every color.

For the uninitiated, a look at where women filmmakers have come from can prove valuable in understanding where they are now and, more important, where they are going. The early history, especially, bears close scrutiny, for in the beginning, lines were drawn and paths were cleared that remain landmarks. My own sense is that even now we have barely begun to emerge, and that a vigorous, multitextured body of work will be appearing in the next decade.

I believe that the development of feminist cinema is tied to the development of the feminist movement, and each has nurtured the other. That is the premise with which this story begins. It is a story I know well, since it is my story too. My life and work have been intertwined with the growth of the feminist film movement from the beginning. This story is being told by a filmmaker, further, by an independent filmmaker. Along the way I will relate my own experiences.

The Dream of Women-controlled Alternative Media

In the late 1960s, as the women's liberation movement was emerging, women could look at the mainstream media and find plenty to be angry about. A major pillar of our critique of sexism was of the images presented to us of ourselves by male-controlled movies and television. When I say male-controlled, I am not kidding. There were no regularly working women directors, executives, or cinematographers and precious few writers and producers. Who were we on the silver screen? Either glamorous objects, asexual mothers, or blond bimbos, all passive characters. When we were active, we were bad: cruel manipulators or heartless seductresses. Our media images were not so different from those in literature or painting: the madonna or the whore. Real thinking, complex women were absent from behind and in front of the camera. Something had to be done.

Women realized that being surrounded by such images was damaging to the spirit. It made us angry; so angry in fact that we said, "Enough!" and set out to find our own course.

Those few of us who looked to work within the industry could not help but notice that television and movies were essentially closed shops. A glance at this history shows that in all the decades of Hollywood, only about five women had directed feature films. Women in decision-making positions in television were practically nonexistent. Some feminists tried to work their way in then. But Hollywood and the networks, with their eyes steadily on the profit line and with their inherent conservatism, did not open their arms to women wanting to tell true stories.

Still, something had to be done. At the close of the 1960s began one of the most yeasty periods for women and film. We were motivated by the radical idea that we had to do it on our own. Often with little training and less experience, young women took cameras and tape recorders into schools, offices, factories, and, especially, kitchens, seeking to document real life and tell true stories. These early films are mostly short, black and white, and lack polish. Even seen today, however, they have a sense of discovery. Like the consciousness-raising groups, all across the United States, that helped women discover who they are individually and collectively, these films are mostly interested in *letting women speak for themselves.* This was a radical act in the 1960s. I would venture a guess that virtually every woman who began making films in this era was part of a consciousness-raising group and deeply affected by it. This focus on unglamorized everyday life and trust in women's personal testimony became cornerstones of feminist filmmaking, and remain so today.

My own film work, with my partner, Jim Klein, began in 1970 with *Growing Up Female.* Made for $2,000 while we were

Antioch College students, the film looks at the ways women are socialized. We chose to depict the lives of six females aged four to thirty-five. When some younger women view *Growing Up Female* today they are sure it must have been made in the 1950s, so blatant is the sexism and so naive the women as to sexism's effects. I patiently explain that when the film was made, the world was very different. Abortion was illegal everywhere in the United States. Unmarried women, practically speaking, did not have access to birth control. The Equal Rights Amendment was not yet in the public eye. Women's Studies was nonexistent. Equal pay for equal work had not yet been raised as a demand. Day care was hard to find. Lesbians were closeted, aside from a few urban enclaves. *Ms* magazine did not exist, nor did women's clinics, women's centers, exhibits of women's art, or girls on Little League teams. Yes, hair and dress styles have changed since then and blatant sexism is not as easily found. Still, the societal processes we depicted in 1970 are still at work today and, for the most part, in the same ways now as then.

Other films of this period are *Janie's Janie* by Geri Ashur, *The Woman's Film* by the Newsreel Collective, *Three Lives* by Kate Millett, *Anything You Want to Be* by Liane Brandon, and *Home Movie* by Jan Oxenberg.

These are all first-step films. They are rueful statements, designed less to entertain (although all have funny sequences) than to activate. And activate they did. It is important to note that the settings in which these films were seen by audiences were also new. Rather than in theaters, on television, or even in college classrooms, women gathered in living rooms, church basements, or the newly forming women's centers to view them. At the back of the room sat the projector. A woman ran it. It was a communal experience, provoking discussion. These films were concretely part of what helped the women's movement grow. They were an attraction we could publicize in the community and to which we could invite our nonfeminist friends. They brought people together and inspired us to action. The very nature of how these early films were made and shown added to their power. The handmade, hands-on quality held powerful messages for women: "We did this! We can do it. Our work doesn't have to be slick, doesn't have to follow *their* rules, to be effective. We are forging our own way." Those were exciting days.

As the movement developed and its philosophy began to be articulated, women's organizations began to look at all aspects of life and question whether the status quo was the best way. We tried to create processes and structures to fight that which had oppressed us: power hierarchies, centralization, competition, and reliance on "experts." We came up with new ways of doing things—of conducting a meeting (rotating the position of chairperson), of leadership (collective), of arriving at decisions (by consensus), of learning (sharing skills), of living (collectively). This was an all-important feminist insight: it is the forms and structures within which we operate that oppress us, that keep us passive and divided. These must be transformed before we can truly change.

Women applied these same questions to all aspects of film: shooting, editing, distribution, and exhibition. In place of the standard hierarchy, with director on top, assistant director underneath, and so on down to lowly and poorly treated production assistants, films were made collectively, with crew positions rotated so all could learn. Editing became a group process. It was assumed that all could learn any skill, technical or creative, not simply those who showed a knack. I learned how to record sound and how to shoot with a 16-mm sync sound camera. It strikes me as unlikely that I would have been encouraged to learn these skills in any era before or since.

I remember well the editing of *Growing Up Female*. One day Jim sat at the editing machine and cut; the next day I did. And so on till the end. He clearly was more facile at it; it was easier for him; he was faster. This never was brought up. In this atmosphere many women who would never have had the chance to overcome their fear of things technical became skilled in filmmaking.

The area of distribution needed changing also. Few, if any, of the existing companies were interested in these films because they could not see them making profit. Besides, they were crudely made. Even when distribution contracts were offered they were unacceptable to feminists. The filmmaker had to give up all rights to her work for many years and had no say over the price to be charged or the publicity to be used. Prices were higher than most women's groups could afford. This would mean that the main audiences for these films would never be reached. My partner and I were in this exact position in 1971 with *Growing Up Female*. Our decision was to distribute the film ourselves. We taught ourselves how, printed a brochure ourselves, and did our first mailing in 1971 under the name New Day Films. It was so successful, with requests pouring in, that we decided to take the idea to two other feminist filmmakers, Liane Brandon and Amalie Rothschild. From the four of us was born the New Day Films Cooperative. It was completely run by the filmmakers. A year later we took on another film, Joyce Chopra and Claudia Weill's *Joyce at 34,* and the co-op has been growing ever since. A similar group, Women Make Movies, was founded in 1975, both to teach filmmaking skills and to distribute films by women.

The First International Festival of Women's Film was organized and held in New York City in 1972. It was a breakthrough event, bringing together filmmakers from all over the United States, Canada, and Europe. One hundred twenty-five films were shown, representing all genres and including all subject matter. Panel discussions were held; critics and academics came; audiences lined up. This was the "debut" of the feminist film movement in the larger world. One reviewer wrote, "Even film scholars were amazed to discover that there were three weeks' worth of films directed by women in existence" (Braderman). The effects of the festival were far-reaching. In her book *Women's Reflections* Jan Rosenberg recalls that

> for quite some time, the program notes of the Festival (widely circulated during the Festival, and mailed to hundreds more who requested them after the Festival was over) were the only published information on feminist films. They were the first comprehensive definition of and guide to this emerging movement; they allowed people who had missed the Festival (teachers, film programmers, filmmakers, critics, etc.) to learn about the films and the film movement. (99)

The First International Festival of Women's Film was followed by fifty or more smaller such festivals across the United States and Canada and by large, government-subsidized festivals in Europe. A second International Festival was held in 1976 in New York City. There has not been a third. For many of us one of the most significant aspects of these festivals was the opportunity to meet filmmakers from other countries and compare notes. I can remember being surprised to learn how many women were making feature films with real budgets in Europe. They all experienced discrimination to be sure. But why were their circumstances so different from ours? We found out. In much of Europe and in Canada, film production is subsidized by the government, not run strictly on the quick profit motive. Under these circumstances a larger measure of democracy enters into decisions about who gets resources for which projects.

Feminist Film Theory and Criticism Emerge

As part of the Second International Festival of Women's Film (1976) there was a significant "first"—the first conference on feminist film scholarship. Topics discussed included women's roles in mainstream movies, ethnicity in women's films, the relationship of cinema *verité* to feminist values, Maya Deren's aesthetic vision, approaches to teaching women and film, and feminist film criticism (Rosenberg 101).

As the final pillar in the foundation I am describing, I want to turn attention to film criticism and theory. At first, feminist critics looked to Hollywood and noted the negative, narrow image of women or the absence of women. They praised films that had strong women characters even if these films were conventionally made. They dealt with film *content* rather than *form*. Then by the late 1970s some critics postulated that we needed a new language in filmmaking, just as we needed new words in spoken language. If "chick" and "baby," "mankind," "Mrs. or Miss," and "chairman" had to go in order to remove language's male bias and its assumption that men are dominant and women secondary, what had to go in film? And what would replace it?

This opened up vast new turf. Women argued that in conventional Hollywood films, everything is seen through male eyes. Of course the director, cinematographer, and probably the writer and all the technicians will be male. But the argument goes farther. Most stories are told from the male point of view. Men are the heroes, the main characters with whom the audience is encouraged to identify. So in every way *the gaze is male.* Women are always seen from the male perspective rather than on their own terms. Even strong women are seen through men's eyes.

Further, women argued, the way cinema is received encourages a passive voyeurism. It encourages the illusion that life is made up of seamless stories with a clear beginning, middle, and end. It creates a world we passively enter and allow to carry us, unthinking, accepting, to the end. It is pleasurable perhaps, but is this passive gaze what feminists want to encourage (Mulvey)? A number of women filmmakers rejected this approach and set out to find new strategies. Filmmakers such as Laura Mulvey, Yvonne Rainer, Chantal Ackerman, and, later, Michelle Citroen and Jill Godmilow created anti-illusionist, antinarrative films. Their work consciously tries to distance us from itself, asking us not to be passively entertained, but actively to put the film together. We are forced to consider, to think about, the roles women play in their films, and about the women's relationships to one another.

It is interesting to note that it was mainly non-U.S. filmmakers who have worked in these experimental forms (Briton Mulvey, Canadian Rainer, and Belgian Ackerman). Perhaps the pull of Hollywood and network television is just that much stronger in the consciousness of U.S. women.

Over time, feminist film critics have explored using psychoanalysis, Marxism, and semiology in grappling with the creation of a feminist aesthetic. Their theories are now commonly taught in university film studies programs and widely written about (see Postscript and Bibliography).

Issue Films, New Audiences

Meanwhile back to my narrative. As the 1970s wore on a new group of films by women began to emerge. They paralleled the next stage of development of the women's movement. These films could be categorized as "issue films." As feminists moved from anger into action we began to define what in society needed changing. Films offering the information we needed, in a feminist perspective, were made on a broad array of subjects—abortion, rape, child care, health concerns, the Equal Rights Amendment, lesbian issues, racial discrimination, union organizing, divorce, and child custody. Most are short and most are documentaries. A steady stream of these films has been (and is being) produced. Generally the skill level is higher than in the first burst of films. We were learning our craft.

The use of films about women was quickly broadening too. This was partly because of our own alternative institutions: Women's Studies on university campuses, women's centers and services, and the occasional feminist in a high school or office. Equally important, feminism was affecting the mainstream. Public libraries bought our films. Corporations became interested. Nonfeminist classroom teachers realized that they needed our perspective in their courses. Museums with exhibition programs and film festivals held regular "films by women" showcases.

Experimental Films

Before the 1960s and through the present, women have made experimental and animated avant-garde films. Their works are harder to classify than issue or portrait films. By nature, they are highly individual artistic expressions. They cannot be analyzed only in terms of their content. These films explore the filmmakers' personal life or the nature of film itself. However, because they are made by women, many deal with common feminist themes, such as sexuality, identity, motherhood, and birth.

Grandmother Movies

By the late 1970s another subgenre of feminist film could not escape notice. I call these the grandmother movies. They are portrait films, often beautifully crafted, often biographies of the filmmakers' mother, grandmother, aunt, or mentor. The filmmakers' urge was to take a new look at the lives of their progenitors and perhaps to search for all-important role models. Examples of this genre are *Yudie* by Mirra Bank; *Old Fashioned Woman* by Martha Coolidge; *Antonia: Portrait of a Woman* by Jill Godmilow, with Judy Collins; *Fundi* by Joanne Grant; *Woo Who, May Wilson* and *Nana, Mom and Me* by Amalie Rothschild; and *Libba Cotten* by Geri Ashur.

In the more introspective late 1970s these more personal works were perhaps more acceptable to programmers and mass audiences than were the earlier genres.

During this time my partner and I produced *Union Maids* (1976), a portrait of three dynamic working-class women who were part of the rank and file labor movement in the 1930s. Although not my actual grandmothers, these three served as forbears to me in shaping my identity as a working-class woman. *Union Maids* was among the first oral history films, followed by many other wonderful examples of this genre: *With Babies and Banners* by Lorraine Gray, Lyn Goldfarb, and Anne Bohlen; *Rosie the Riveter* by Connie Field; *The Wobblies* by Deborah Shaffer and Stewart Bird; and so on. These history films were being created at the same time as feminist historians were doing their ground-breaking work. Using the novel methods needed to examine the largely unrecorded activities of women in the past, they pored over diaries, letters, shopping lists, checkbooks, oral testimony, etc. In my view the same impetus propelled the historians, the more personal "grandmother films," and these more political "oral history" films: the desire to know and celebrate our roots.

But another, less hopeful reason propelled women filmmakers to look to the past and also helped to set the stage for the next wave of feminist films. That was the waning of 1960s activism, the setbacks in women's rights, and the general societal drift toward conservatism and complacency. By the beginning of the 1980s there seemed to be fewer burning issues, fewer struggles to document. The future was uncertain. It was a hard time for leftists of all stripes, a time of looking to earlier movements for clues and inspiration. Our most recent film,

Seeing Red, is a product of this era. It is a feature-length documentary about individuals who joined the Communist party in the 1930s and their lives until now.

Hard realities set in. Filmmakers found that audiences for militant films were shrinking. Public television became less interested in hard-hitting documentaries. Grants and other support for political films, never plentiful, began to dry up in the Reagan years. There are many ways those in political power can alter the cultural hegemony.

These factors and several others—established filmmakers' natural desire for new challenges, larger audiences, and more recognition; the upsurge of cable television and its appetite for new entertainment products; and the general invigoration of the independent feature-film community—ushered in the current era, when undoubtedly the big news is the presence of women directors and producers on near-mainstream movies.

Women Filmmakers of Color

If women as a group are underrepresented in film images and on film crews, women of color are grossly underrepresented. The racism of Hollywood is harsher than its sexism. Even in the more flexible, open independent film world few Third World voices are heard. Of course this is partly due to women of racial minorities having extremely limited access to resources. It must be said that the majority of women filmmakers are from upper-middle-class backgrounds. Their parents were able to give them the education and sense of confidence needed to enter the daunting field of filmmaking. Often family money paid for their early work. It is rare to find a Third World woman in this situation. Still, a strong group of women of color have managed to produce excellent work—women such as Christine Choy *(Mississippi Triangle* and *To Love, Honor, and Obey)*, Julie Dash *(Illusions* and *Four Women)*, Ayoka Chenzira *(Hair Piece: A Film for Nappyheaded People)*, Kathleen Collins *(Losing Ground)*, Anna Maria Garcia *(La Operacion)*, Joanne Grant *(Fundi: The Story of Ella Barker)*, Alile Sharon Larkin *(A Different Image* and *Your Children Come Back to You)*, Jackie Shearer *(A Minor Altercation)*,

Silvia Morales *(Chicana)*, Michelle Parkinson *(Gotta Make This Journey* and . . . *but then, she's Betty Carter)*, and Lourdes Portillo *(Las Madres* and *After the Earthquake)*. These women have brought to audiences stories that the dominant white media could not. Third World women have generally chosen to produce or distribute their work under the auspices of organizations founded and run by minority filmmakers—for example, Third World Newsreel, The Black Filmmaker Foundation, and Asian CineVision.

Feature Films, Box Office Success

Beginning with sporadic, but significant work in the late 1970s—*Girlfriends* (Claudia Weill), *Hester Street* (Joan Micklin Silver), *Valley Girls* (Martha Coolidge), *Fast Times at Ridgemont High* (Amy Heckerling)—but not gaining steam till the mid-1980s, women in the independent and Hollywood worlds have been directing feature fiction work for movie theater distribution. In Hollywood, working within the system, Coolidge, Weill, Silver, Jane Wagner *(Moment by Moment)*, Joan Tewksbury *(Old Boyfriends)*, and Randa Haines *(Children of a Lesser God)* have directed respected films. Still, the greater body of work, and the body of work that bears the filmmakers' individual visions, comes from outside the system. The live question now is, can women retain their vision and control of their work, and yet put together the resources and raise the money to make films for mass audiences?

A note on the word money is important here. Shorter, earlier films by women were made on relatively low budgets, from under $10,000 to no more than $150,000. This money was generally raised by grants and donations. The price tag for making good-looking feature films begins at a rock bottom of $500,000, but much more commonly runs from $1 million to $3 million. And I am speaking of low-budget, independent features. Sums like this can be raised only by *investment*. That is, it is expected that the money will be paid back, with interest.

We can begin to discern our answer. Recently a number of independently made films directed and mostly written by women have appeared. Because they are independent films we know that they represent the vision of the director. These directors were not assigned to do them. They struggled and fought to bring them to life. Most are stories about female life— *Smooth Talk* by Joyce Chopra, *Desert Hearts* by Donna Deitch, *Twelve Minutes in Heaven* by Linda Fefferman, *Working Girls* by Lizzie Borden, *Desperately Seeking Susan* by Susan Seidelman, *Testament* by Lynne Littman, and *Waiting for the Moon* by Jill Godmilow.

Almost every director in this list has been making films for many years; their credits appear on the earliest of feminist films. Their aesthetic approach was shaped in the era of consciousness-raising groups. They have paid their dues and matured their skills for a long time. Now they are strong enough to hold on to their visions. Also, alternative means of financing low-budget features have been hammered out over the years. Major studios are no longer the only route to financing and mounting features. Instead, an array of possibilities exists: Public Broadcasting System's American Playhouse, the Sundance Institute, European television networks, art film distributors, and limited-investment partnerships.

Hollywood Beckons

With a successful independent feature to their credit, these directors are getting calls from Hollywood studios or major independent studios (De Laurentis, Cannon) to consider making films with studio backing and, of course, studio control. Here the plot thickens. Not having to scrape around for financing or distribution is awfully tempting. The opportunity to make films on larger budgets ($5 million and up) with major stars is hard to pass up. Will our heroine be able to hold her ground? Or will the moguls gradually sap her strength and lead her to bargain away her personal vision? Will women be able to make it in Hollywood on their own terms?

Will women in any numbers make it there at all? Will we be able to transform the image factory? I remain profoundly doubtful. By the late 1990s we may know the answers to these questions, but I, for one, prefer the tortuous independent route. Our budgets may be much smaller and the task longer. But in the end we know who we are. And we know what our work stands for. And after all, that's why we got into this in the first place: to create work that makes a difference.

Postscript and Bibliography

With all the focus in the late 1980s on women as feature directors it might be easy to conclude that theirs is the only game in town. Not so. I take the risk of mentioning only a few of the scores of recent works. We are still producing high-quality issue films such as *The Global Assembly Line* by Lorraine Gray, *Las Madres* by Susana Muñoz and Lourdes Portillo, *Broken Rainbow* by Victoria Mudd; historical films such as *The International Sweethearts of Rhythm* by Greta Schiller and Andrea Weiss, *The Flapper Story* by Louise Lazin, *Are We Winning Mommy?* by Barbara Margolis, *Women of Summer* by Suzanne Bauman and Rita Heller; films that combine personal and political stories such as *Metropolitan Avenue* by Christine Noschese, *Gotta Make This Journey* by Michelle Parkinson, and *You Got to Move* by Lucy Massie Phenix; and wonderful animated or experimental works such as *Nexus* by Rose Bond and *Voices* by Joanna Priestly. The following bibliography provides further information. Most of these books contain much more extensive bibliographies than I could present here.

Betancourt, Jeanne. *Women in Focus*. Dayton, OH: Pflaum Publishing, 1974.
Doane, Mary Ann, Patricia Mellencamp, and Linda Williams. *Re-Vision: Essays in Feminist Film Criticism*. Frederick, MD: American Film Institute Monograph Series, 1984.
Foreman, Alexa L. *Women in Motion*. Bowling Green, OH: Bowling Green University Popular Press, 1983.
Gentile, Mary C. *Film Feminisms: Theory and Practice*. Westport, CT: Greenwood Press, 1985.
Haskell, Molly. *From Reverence to Rape: The Treatment of Women in the Movies*. New York: Holt, Rinehart & Winston, 1973.

Kaplan, E. Ann. *Women and Film: Both Sides of the Camera*. New York: Methuen, 1983.

Kuhn, Annette. *Women's Pictures: Feminism and Cinema*. Boston: Routledge and Kegan Paul, 1982.

Rosen, Marjorie. *Popcorn Venus*. New York: Coward, McCann & Geoghegan, 1973.

Rosenberg, Jan. *Women's Reflections: The Feminist Film Movement*. Ann Arbor, MI: UMI Research Press, 1983.

Works Cited

Braderman, Joan. *Art Forum* 11 (1972):87.

"Ms. Treatment." *Film Comment* 21 (1985):20–25.

Mulvey, Laura. "Visual Pleasures and Narrative Cinema." *Screen* 16 (1975):6–18.

Rosenberg, Jan. *Women's Reflections: The Feminist Film Movement*. Ann Arbor, MI: UMI Research Press, 1983.

CHAPTER 6

Gender and the Economy
Women in the "Free-Market Family"

LINDA C. MAJKA

A COMMON PICTURE of the economy is that it is the place where men earn a family wage while women are at home doing housework and bringing up children. The fact that most women's lives differ substantially from this image does not seem to influence the expectation that men are to be the sole providers in families and women are to be dependent on men in marriage, under their guardianship and control. Current feminist scholarship emphasizes that these traditional expectations are socially constructed rather than biologically inevitable. This chapter is concerned with eliminating myths about gender roles in the family and the economy. It is specifically focused on economic ideas that have gained prominence during the Reagan administration. A critical perspective is necessary because governmental policies have been based on traditional assumptions about gender roles. Also, the ability of citizens to make the changes needed in the economy and the family depends on an awareness of the importance of economic independence for women.

The recent popularization of economic ideas supporting the concept of free-market capitalism carries with it powerful images of how gender relationships and American families are and ought to be. Four widely publicized recent books offer interpretations for popular audiences of the economic principles that influence the Reagan administration; at the same time they promote implicitly and sometimes directly a remarkably consistent version of what should be celebrated and condemned in contemporary gender relationships and families. Although the authors differ in their proposals for the best route to a new prosperity in America, they are near consensus on matters regarding gender and families. In this respect supply-side proponents, such as George Gilder, Jack Kemp, and Jude Wanniski, are linked with monetarist economist Milton Friedman and his wife and coauthor, Rose Friedman.

The academic intellectual communities have focused their attention on these authors' economic ideas. All are considered major sources on free-market economics and have become major sales successes. *Wealth and Poverty,* by George Gilder, is an international best-seller and resulted in television appearances by the author as well as the opportunity to write speeches for President Reagan. *An American Renaissance,* by Jack Kemp, is reviewed in literary and academic journals as well as in business and popular magazines. Although not a professional economist, Jude Wanniski succeeded in getting his book, *The Way the World Works,* reviewed internationally in economics journals and magazines. Milton Friedman, Nobel laureate and possibly the world's most famous conservative economist, had a ten-part television series for the Public Broadcasting System before publishing the related book, *Free to Choose.* All the authors receive lavish praise in business publications. Scholarly critics are decidedly more reserved, but most generally treat them as well deserving of serious consideration. Academic reviewers also differ from journalists in their willingness to acknowledge that the books show a casual, and even exploitative, attitude toward scholarship.

The frequent reviews in business and academic publications give primary attention to the authors' economic theories but almost no systematic evaluation of their statements about gender and families. The critics' principal reservations focus on the nature of the economic models, such as whether the "Laffer curve" is correct. Their infrequent references to the authors' assumptions and arguments concerning gender and the family either take the form of descriptions or imply at least a cautious acceptance of the basic propositions.

To redress this omission, this chapter identifies some of the areas of agreement among authors Gilder, Kemp, Wanniski, and the Friedmans concerning gender and families. To analyze thoroughly the merits and shortcomings of their arguments and document the research that would validate or reject their claims would take a much longer study. But it is possible here to examine the regularities in their central assumptions, survey some of the evidence that raises questions about their fundamental propositions, and give some reasons why their ideas have attracted so much favorable attention.

Three major themes inform supply-side assumptions on the linkages between the economy, on one hand, and gender and family, on the other. The authors agree first that the social welfare system weakens the family as an institution as well as attacks the economic fabric of society. Second, they argue that "free" (or deregulated) labor markets are necessary to strengthen the position of men in families. Finally, they assume that the best tactic to reach a more prosperous future is to channel resources to the men in those families who are already affluent.

Welfare and Families

There is a striking unanimity among the authors with respect to state provision of welfare services. The consensus is neatly summarized by Jack Kemp, a former quarterback for the Buffalo Bills, who has, since 1970, been a U.S. representative from a blue-collar district in New York. In his book *An American Renaissance,* essentially a homage to the old American dream of personal upward mobility through individual effort, he tells us:

> The American people consider themselves a kind of extended family. . . . We are repelled by the thought of ignoring genuine suffering. . . . Yet because people want this safety net in place, it doesn't follow that they therefore want it filled up with sufferers. Least of all do they want their assistance to seduce others into habits of dependency. (78)

This statement resonates with a deep-seated American sentiment. For example, in *Middletown in Transition* (1937), Robert and Helen Lynd recorded a similar belief. In the midst of the Depression those expressing the "Middletown Spirit" adopted a mood of human kindliness, while at the same time denouncing the "government dole" because "a paternalistic system which prescribes an exact method of aiding our unfortunate brothers and sisters is demoralizing." Further, "it undermines a man's character for him to get what he doesn't earn" (415). In Middletown it was more worthy to give aid than to receive it: the donor was admired, the client despised as "too lazy to work, too spendthrift to save, too shortsighted to plan" (415). As the Lynds observed in the 1930s, the attitudes were designed to flatter the business elite at the expense of the lower classes.

Fifty years later Jude Wanniski, a former *Wall Street Journal* editorial writer, explains why social welfare is economically unsound. In *The Way the World Works* he argues: "Americans get welfare benefits, and to a greater degree, retirement benefits, explicitly on the condition that they be unemployed" (95). By making these payments available the government "crushes out incentives and underemploys an entire economy" (96). According to Wanniski's economic model, if a government wants to increase production, it can accomplish this by making unemployment less attractive, "first by reducing unemployment subsidies (welfare benefits)" and "then by increasing non-work penalties," including government harassment and even "threatening physical punishment, imprisonment, slavery, etc." (84). Wanniski confirms the recent arguments by Piven and Cloward that the intention behind contemporary attacks on income-maintenance programs is the desire to force people to sell their labor at or below what they need to secure necessities (28).

Milton Friedman and Rose Friedman state unambiguously in their book *Free to Choose* that America is divided into two classes: "one receiving relief and the other paying for it" (107). They argue that "most of the present welfare programs should never have been enacted. If they had not been, many of the people now dependent on them would have become self-reliant individuals instead of wards of the state" (119). Social programs should be eliminated because they "weaken the family; reduce the incentive to work, save and innovate; reduce the accumulation of capital; and limit our freedom" (127).

The Friedmans' book offers no convincing evidence that the current structure of income-maintenance programs is more destructive of family life than exposure to the hardships of an unregulated market economy. Piven and Cloward offer the persuasive rebuttal that to eliminate welfare at a time when there are few other economic and social opportunities is clearly a worse solution because the results for families will be to make economic insecurity more intense for the unemployed and the working poor, and to create additional unemployment as more women, teenagers, and elderly are forced into the labor market (32–33). Research findings confirm increased hardships for years after Congress passed the Omnibus Budget Reconciliation Act in 1981 at the request of the Reagan administration. The law eliminated cash supplements, Food Stamps, Medicaid insurance, housing, emergency assistance, eligibility for child care, and work-related expenses for employed women with children who received AFDC ("welfare"). Women in these families perceived that their social and economic circumstances had considerably declined since 1982, and many reported almost continual crises. They suffered increased indebtedness, problems in health and child care, changes in residence, and even homelessness (Sarri).

The proposition that welfare undermines the family is developed more completely by George Gilder than by the other popular writers on free-market economics. His book *Wealth and Poverty* ranked high on best-seller lists for months and was approvingly displayed by Ronald Reagan on national television. Harvard sociologist Nathan Glazer allowed his endorsement of the book to be printed on the jacket of the 1981 hardback edition, giving the book the veneer of scholarly respectability.

In the book Gilder states that "welfare . . . exerts a constant, seductive, erosive pressure on the marriages and work habits of the poor" (122). The principal means by which welfare weakens the family is through its impact on the husband/father. The studies that examine poverty and unemployment as the major sources of family breakdown, according to Gilder, fail to recognize the underlying, but less measurable factors: levels of "male confidence and authority, which determine sexual potency, respect from the wife and children, and motivation" (114). The assumption here is that "male confidence and authority" are the causal variables. In other words, Gilder accepts male domination as natural and ties normal sexual activity to the provider role. No researchers, however, have any hypotheses, let alone data, to support any assertion as to what level of male authority might be associated with what level of sexual potency.

As Gilder continues, because of welfare the man feels "that his role as provider, the definitive male activity from the primal days of the hunt . . . has been largely seized from him" (115). Man the hunter is not to be denied: he responds with "resignation and rage, escapism and violence, short horizons and promiscuous sexuality that characterizes everywhere the life of the poor" (115). Gilder is not concerned about the spread of this behavior among the idle rich, and fails to document its existence among the diverse segments of the poor. He also neglects anthropological evidence on the families of our human ancestors that shows women customarily provided for their families by gathering and sharing food. In fact, women provided two to three times as much food by weight as did men, since gathering plants was a more reliable source of protein than hunting animals (Osmond).

Gilder argues in other writings that in our society, welfare money and other social services are a right given to women by the state, and they "enhance" the mother's role in the family to the detriment of the father (115–22). Gilder is assuming that the interests of the two genders are automatically in opposition: what is beneficial to women is harmful to men. He fails to note what has been evident for some time, that living in female-maintained families exacts a high penalty from women and children, even with the financial support of welfare (Ross 153; Bernard 246).

Gilder is familiar with the study by Heather Ross and Isabel Sawhill in which the connection between welfare and family breakdown is examined. In *Time of Transition* Ross and Sawhill did a comprehensive appraisal of available data on female-headed families and found no evidence that welfare encourages marital separation. These are conclusions Gilder will not accept, and instead, in a footnote, he mentions the researchers' observation that AFDC has a role in delaying remarriage among its recipients. Also, he notes their prediction that a broadened income-maintenance program would stabilize marriage among low-income whites and nonwhites (Ross and Sawhill 162), but he dismisses their findings and conclusions on the grounds that these analyses ignore the "profound male need to perform the provider role" (278).

If the absence of well-paid socially useful and meaningful work offends the human dignity of men, why would it not also affront women? Data on the hardships that women experience during their unemployment (Schlozman) contradict Gilder's assertion that a woman's family responsibilities cause her to lack the "all-out commitment" required by full-time employment (69). Gilder traces women's supposed disinterest in their jobs to the observation that female sexuality "is psychologically rooted in the bearing and nurturing of children" (70). He spares the reader any doubt that his justifications for women's subordinate economic status are based on anything less than physical characteristics.

To those who believe that institutional racism and discrimination play a large part in accounting for the disproportionately low incomes of minorities, Gilder replies, "Nothing is more deadly to achievement than the belief that effort will not be rewarded, that the world is a bleak and discriminatory place" (69). He thus sidesteps the real problem: it is not that the reward structure for nonwhites is absent, but that it is different. Numerous analysts have shown that racial inequality remains a fundamental element in the social class structure of the United States. Blacks continue to be concentrated in occupations with lower incomes and status than those of whites. Dramatic gains in educational attainment by blacks in recent decades have not produced comparable improvements in incomes. Also, status mobility achieved by one generation of black families cannot be passed on to their children to the same extent as for whites.

The central problem with welfare, in Gilder's view, is that benefits are pegged at levels that are higher than prevailing wages and productivity levels in poor communities. He advocates lowering of the real worth of benefits through allowing inflation to reduce their monetary value (something that is already occurring). It is hard to see how poverty would be lessened if the value of alternative forms of subsistence is allowed to fall. There is ample reason to believe that prevailing wages can be expected to drop still further below what is needed to support dependents in the absence of contrary pressure from income-maintenance programs. When employed women with children were removed from AFDC in 1981, they were unable to provide necessities, especially child care and medical care, because they had very low wages and few or no benefits in their jobs. Many faced serious crises, such as running out of money and food, serious illnesses, death, job loss, family violence, and problems with children. Lack of money took the greatest toll on their physical and mental health, and poor health was linked with the inability to remain employed. When these women lost their jobs they were forced back on AFDC at higher costs and for lengthier periods (Sarri).

Most of the assertions made by Gilder (as well as by the other authors) about welfare, work, gender, and the family are insufficiently supported with research evidence. Where citations exist they typically refer to their own publications or Harvard's Edward Banfield and Thomas Sowell. More often the reader is expected to recognize what the authors apparently assume are "self-evident truths." Gilder does, however, make use of a study by Irwin Garfinkel and Robert Haveman as major support for his proposition that "the only dependable route from poverty is always work, family, and faith. The first principle is that in order to move up, the poor must not only work, they must work harder than the classes above them" (68).

It is worth examining in detail what the cited poverty research by Garfinkel and Haveman *actually* said. Funded by the Institute for Research on Poverty at the University of Wisconsin, the study was designed to analyze poverty by measuring "earnings capacity," that is, "the income stream that would be generated if a household unit employed its human and physical assets to capacity" (8). It also measured earnings "capacity utilization rates," that is, the "ratio of actual earnings to earnings capacity, where earnings capacity is adjusted for limitations on work resulting from illness, disability, and unemployment but does not include a family's nonemployment income" (28). The authors of the cited monograph reported that their results "indicate that low utilization of earnings capacity plays a relatively minor role in explaining the general problem of poverty" (34). Stated differently, the incidence of poverty is not well explained by differences in the work effort of individuals and groups.

The Wisconsin authors also argue that "this evidence provides *no support for the hypothesis that the high incidence of poverty among blacks and other population subgroups is primarily attributable to their failure to exploit economic potential*" (35; italics added). In this respect, the results are closer to being supportive of arguments made about poverty by Christopher Jencks and colleagues and Lester Thurow. They recognize that current levels of income inequality in the United States cannot be attributed to such factors as work effort (Thurow 202) and job competence (Jencks 263), views that Gilder is anxious to dismiss. The Wisconsin authors' conclusions are in no way casual observations, but are given a prominent place in their analysis of findings. A review of their monograph leaves little doubt that, by quoting out of context, Gilder promoted a systematic misinterpretation of this published research.

On the question of the influence of labor market discrimination on poverty, the Wisconsin authors reported findings that directly contradict Gilder's thesis. They forcefully stated that "racial differences in earnings cannot be attributed to racial differences in the utilization of earnings capacity" (34). As their findings demonstrate, labor market discrimination "accounts for from 43% to 60% of the total earnings gap between black and white males. If labor market discrimination were eliminated, the earnings of black men would increase by 25% to 35%" (90). According to their estimates, if labor market discrimination by race were eliminated, "the earnings of black families would increase by between 24% and 30%. Similarly, between 30% and 39% of the total gap in earnings between black and white families is attributable to labor market discrimination" (84). The conclusions of Garfinkel and Haveman thus contradict Gilder's assertions that "at a time when it is hard to find discrimination anywhere, blacks are being induced to see it everywhere" (138).

As for the lower earnings capacity utilization of married women, the Wisconsin authors found no need to resort, like Gilder, to notions of biological inevitability. Their explanation of the relatively low earnings of women is more empirically grounded (if mundane): "their child care and homemaking activities do not pass through a market and are not rewarded with earned income" (26–27). If a market value were attributed to women's child care and other nonmarket work in the home, the differences between women's earnings and their earnings capacity would be substantially reduced. This explanation of the earnings gap is, however, much less stimulating than Gilder's own view, based on his novel version of female sexuality and "the neurophysiological demands of the sex act itself" (136).

Free Markets and Family Security

The supply-side analysts are unanimous in arguing that free and deregulated labor markets are necessary for economic well-being. Unrestrained labor market competition creates the most appropriate context for family decisions about who will seek employment. Recognizing that public policy has had an important part in regulating the labor force, the authors aim their primary complaints at minimum wage laws, unemployment compensation, and social security retirement benefits.

Jack Kemp tersely argues the case against the minimum wage: "Of all the barriers to opportunity imposed by government, I can think of few more onerous than the minimum wage law, for it arrests the natural development of young people at a crucial stage" (43); this occurs by taking "the bottom rungs off the opportunity ladder" (44). The Friedmans argue that "the minimum wage law requires employers to discriminate against persons with low skills" (237). The government penalizes young people, especially blacks, "by preventing them from offering to work for low wages as a means of inducing employers to give them on-the-job training" (238).

It is typical for the authors to make their policy recommendations without any recognition that some families would be worse off if minimum wages were eliminated. Presumably, young people who now have minimum wage jobs would have to work longer hours to keep up their earnings if their wages were allowed to fall by eliminating the minimum wage. Families with only two breadwinners might find the addition of a third a necessity. Before the 1938 Fair Labor Standards Act (the federal wage and hour law) the employment of wives and children of low-paid workers was the norm (Brody 21). Without minimum wage protection the income added to the working-class family economy by these workers with weak bargaining power did not result in even an adequate standard of living under urban conditions. There is no logical prospect that the removal of minimum wage standards would restore or create the sole-provider role, as claimed.

When the auto industry and related manufacturing industries declined in the 1970s, many highly paid jobs that employed men disappeared, perhaps permanently. In the 1980s the only way many households collect a "family wage" is "by adding up the wages of individual family members—husbands, wives and often grown children as well" (Ehrenreich 173). The minimum wage has failed to keep up with inflation, not to speak of improving the real wages of the lowest paid workers. In 1985 the minimum wage was only $3.35: in real terms this is 8 percent below the 1960 level and more than 23 percent below the 1974 level. If a person worked forty hours a week, fifty-two weeks a year, at the minimum wage in 1985, his or her annual earnings would be only $6,968 (Winnick). These annual earnings are minimally adequate to support an adult in an urban area and totally inadequate if shared with a dependent.

The free-market publicists give us no data to support their assumption that extremely low paid work offers training that is translated into upward mobility. In fact, unskilled jobs have changed dramatically over this century; now such jobs do *not* lead to upward mobility on a continuous "opportunity ladder." Even in the past, low wages did not automatically lead to on-the-job training for better work. For example, when wages were extremely low, employers could expect workers to spend part of their time on the job idle and waiting for orders or materials because their labor time was so cheap (Montgomery 37–40). Family income did not, therefore, increase because of the upward mobility of the employed father. Instead, as children reached employment age, they left school early and entered paid work to raise family income.

The Friedmans treat unemployment compensation as simply another form of welfare that contributes, by definition, to weakening the family. Wanniski also complains that countercyclical spending on unemployment benefits by the government encourages workers to find it "increasingly beneficial to be unemployed rather than employed" (233). These authors neglect the fact that employers have profited from the willingness of workers to maintain active job searches, required as a condition for receiving unemployment benefits. Also, they ignore an observation that is commonplace among those who are unemployed, that it is far easier to maintain performance on a given job than it is to seek out and get replacement work.

The Friedmans are especially critical of social security. They complain that it is compulsory and impersonal, and they assert that when it comes to care of the elderly, "moral responsibility is an individual matter, not a social matter." They regret the passing of the time when "children helped their parents out of love or duty" but now "contribute to the support of someone else's parents out of compulsion and fear" (106). Again, we are told that transfer payments for retirement and old age weaken the bonds of the family. It is implied that those elderly who find themselves without other resources would be "free" to compete in a deregulated labor market. Presumably, they would be able to support themselves.

Because the authors provide little or no evidence that the existence of the legislation that established the minimum wage, unemployment compensation, and social security system weakens the family, their assessment of family impact is more likely a rationalization for policy conclusions they were predisposed to make, rather than a basis for them (cf. Pankhurst and Houseknecht 24–25). The real reason behind the authors' objections to the legislation appears to be that it is a hallmark of free-market economics to assert that governmental activity should be reduced and market activity encouraged. They oppose forms of public regulation that interfere with the voluntary and so-called natural process of labor market exchanges and infringe on the freedoms of corporate property and prerogatives of management.

There is an alternative view of economic freedom: it can also take the form of laws that set people free from the hardships of the marketplace (Heilbroner 6; Tyler 289). After all, the exchange of labor for wages is not nearly as voluntary as the authors proclaim. People sell their labor under prevailing conditions of imbalances in market power that favor employers over workers. Especially in occupations that are unorganized or have weak unions, people are unable to protect themselves against injurious changes in working conditions and wages, sanctioned by a sluggish economy with high unemployment. Women's rights to equal dignity and economic well-being are problematic even in the best of times. During the recessions of the Reagan administration women experienced higher rates of long-term unemployment, underemployment, and job discouragement compared with men. Women were segregated into jobs that were sex-typed, low-paying, and insecure. Discrimination caused a lag in earnings relative to men and, for many women, led to poverty (Majka 102–4). Also, the gap between the rich and the poor grew wider, and racial inequalities worsened during the Reagan years. The incidence of poverty among blacks and Hispanics was many times that experienced among whites. The distribution of wealth by race was even more inequitable than income. This increased the vulnerability of nonwhite families when they experienced employment insecurity (Winnick).

Policy prescriptions for economic recovery emanating from free-market economics place greater constraint on the mass of people than on elites. Monetarism intends to solve economic stagnation by recession, mass unemployment, widespread business bankruptcies and foreclosures, and a drawn-out slow recovery. Supply-siders propose to encourage savings, enlarge output, and increase productivity by generous amounts of credit, low interest rates, and massive military spending (Lekachman 172). Both endorse tax cuts for the affluent, increasing worker insecurity, and shifts of public resources from the poor and unemployed into higher business profits and capital accumulation (Ackerman 17–18). On such policy matters diverse conservative schools are in agreement; for example, neoconservative writers associated with the American Enterprise Institute, like Irving Kristol and Michael Novak, arrive at many of the same policy prescriptions from different economic assumptions (Majka, "Perspectives"). In fact, the massive tax cuts of the Reagan administration did not move business to invest in industrial equipment: capital spending actually *declined* after the tax breaks (Bowles, Gordon, and Weisskopf 185). Plant closures, high rates of job loss, and farm foreclosures continue amid record federal deficits and business spending on mergers and speculation that add nothing to modernization and employment.

The attack on the regulated labor market returns us to the hazards of the free market, the very economic context in which the popular demand for governmental regulation arose in the first place (Heilbroner 4; Arrow 27). As Piven and Cloward argue, the emergence of free-market capitalism was a violent process, forcing social displacement along with material expansion. The current economic crisis reflects a renewed attempt to reduce the share of national output that goes to the working class (13). Cuts in income-maintenance programs limit the bargaining power of workers and alter the terms on which people will sell their labor (28). The social and political arrangements that maintain capital accumulation are nevertheless less unstable. The unwelcome alliance between the state and property cannot escape the risk that the popular belief in a democratic political order will, in the future, be extended to the economic order. The free-market authors argue its principal defense: they denounce any kind of social reconstruction by nonelites, whether it be access to the law, employment, subsistence, or equal dignity.

Economic Prosperity and Household Income

Whatever their differences on economic philosophy, all the authors agree that the best means of securing a more prosperous future is to direct resources to the affluent segments of the society. Kemp plainly explains that economic expansion "can only come by inviting the strongest, ablest members of society to pull harder by rewarding, not punishing them for their efforts" (80). The strategy to increase production is outlined by Wanniski, and echoed by the Friedmans and Gilder: to eliminate the burdens of regulation and taxation on the affluent and capitalist class.

Concretely the results of such a policy imply a redistribution of resources. The Friedmans' recommendations require a shift of income from the old and the young to the middle-aged who are already secure in their economic positions. Thus they favor a shift of income from the lowest levels of the working class to the business elite, the net effects of the type of tax cuts and social spending cuts they advocate (Pechman; Edsall; Piven and Cloward; Lekachman).

Gilder agrees with these transfers and proposes as well that there be a redistribution from minority groups to the majority, and from women to men. The ability of women to be bread-winners presents particular problems for Gilder. Among blacks, employed women earn 80 percent of the incomes of men, whereas among whites, women earn 60 percent of men's incomes. He argues, "Because of the long evolutionary experience of the race in hunting societies, the provider role accords with the deepest instincts of men" (136).

The solution, according to Gilder, is to lower the incomes of black *women,* to produce an earnings gap comparable to the pattern for white men and women. He would also eliminate the "unfair" situation created by the two-earner family: that is, "two half-hearted participants in the labor force can do better than one who is competing aggressively for the relatively few jobs in the upper echelons" (14). This statement gives us a clue to Gilder's idea about how much inequality is "necessary" to society: one man employed in a high-status occupation should earn more than *two* workers in lower-status jobs.

Once again it is important to examine the sources cited by Gilder as validation for his notion that discrimination is a myth. He writes: "Black women face no net current discrimination" (135). The source he cites is the previously described work by Garfinkel and Haveman. An examination of their actual findings reveals that, far from announcing the end of discrimination, Garfinkel and Haveman found that "if labor market discrimination were eliminated the earnings of black women would increase by 19%" (84). Furthermore, the effects of racial discrimination are severer for black women with low skills: "The elimination of labor market discrimination would lead to an increase of 45% in the earnings of black women in the first quintile (of earnings capacity)" (88). Given the increasing numbers of black households headed by women, the impact of continued racial discrimination in labor markets is nothing short of tragic.

The combined effects of racial and sex discrimination on female heads of households contribute to the trend known as the "feminization of poverty": a majority of all poor families with children are now maintained by women (Pearce). No amount of work effort on the part of these women heading households will reduce their poverty and need for welfare as long as they face very low wages in the labor market (Sawhill 206; Shortridge 495–96). Instead, the policy implication is obvious: they should have access to as much income on the job as do men.

The Nuclear Family and the Rise of Capitalism

The foundation for Gilder's policy recommendations is his assessment of the key to the American system of stratification: the fundamental principle of upward mobility in our society is monogamous marriage and family (69). Poverty is a result of "familial anarchy" among the inner-city poor (71). The lower class stagnates because of a "lack of family structure." In contrast to the prosperous middle and entrepreneurial classes, in the lower class "men's links to children and future are too often insufficient to induce work and thrift" (71).

Gilder leaves little doubt that the nuclear family is the key to his larger theory of history. He asserts that the nuclear family "facilitated the long-term development of the highly motivated industrial bourgeoisie and work force" (72). Marriage is central to a man's attitude toward saving and capital. Conversely poverty is a result of illegitimacy and family breakdown because men lack a future orientation that children ensure (72).

Remarkably and regrettably Gilder claims that support for this unexpected thesis on the rise of capitalism is derived from the work of British demographer Edward Anthony Wrigley. Gilder interprets Wrigley to have argued that the emergence of "direct and exclusive links to children in the nuclear family was a prerequisite of the industrial revolution" (71). In contrast, preindustrial men lived in the compass of extended families and did not have to support their children by themselves. Consequently their lives were preoccupied with the present time and short-term prospects. In contrast, industrial men were motivated by "firm links between work, wealth, sex, and children" (72). In other words, the rise of capitalism was caused by man's desire to enrich his nuclear family.

However convenient it may be to Gilder to announce scholarly support for his historical theory that the status of the rich arises from commitment to family structure and that of the poor arises from commitment to family anarchy, it is necessary to reject his view. A more accurate reading of Wrigley's works shows that there was, in fact, no necessary connection between the industrial revolution and the emergence of the modern nuclear family (along with other elements of the complex called "modernization") ("Process" 259). The rise of real wages per capita that was the defining characteristic of industrialization was only a possible—and by no means necessary—outcome of the emergence of the modern nuclear family (244). Stated differently, a society might undergo a transformation in which it substituted the modern nuclear family for the traditional one without also becoming industrialized (237). The decline in traditional family rights and obligations of kinship had no necessary link to economic growth (241).

Self-interest alone, whether based on the individual or widened to the nuclear family, was insufficient to cause rising real incomes. Instead, Wrigley attributed the productivity gains of the industrial revolution in England in large part to technological advances (247). In fact, technical innovation in core capitalist societies broke the connection that had been assumed to exist between living standards and population density. The powers of production were capable of geometric growth, whereas the reproductive means of women and men were relatively modest. Industrialization made it possible to achieve *both* steadily rising real incomes and increasing population (*Population and History,* 54–55).

Far from necessarily creating the industrial revolution, the emergence of the nuclear family resulted in tension with the economic and social changes that accompanied it. The real relationship between industrialization and modernization (changes in the family included) was actually uneasy. Economic transformation had many undesirable consequences for families and communities. The larger postindustrial economic base and personal freedom from traditional restrictions came at a high price: they created both greater misery and greater possibilities for future improvement, but only if their benefits could be equitably distributed.

Conclusion

It is important to understand that free-market ideas emerge from existing social conditions. There is a usefulness in the fact that in their more extreme statements, the authors make global promises with unconditional conviction. History will be brought to a culmination. People will improve everyday life and be united in the unfolding of an immense destiny through "work, family, and faith." The authors' display of a pronounced disdain for social science, empirical evidence, careful logic, and objectivity has a practical explanation.

We are asked to accept on faith the notion that individual motivation, individual consciousness, and individual commitment to traditional values control the future of society. By subverting the idea of social responsibility and social morality they undermine the basis for a moral evaluation of society. They consciously blur the distinction between decision-makers and victims, exploiters and the exploited. The result is twofold. First, morality is a private rather than a social matter. Second, an authoritarian solution to the problem of social order is justified: the use of rewards for the affluent and punishments for the mass of people.

Social scientific investigation offers us the crucial insight that motivation, personal commitments and attachments, and family structures are shaped by existing social and economic circumstances. If personal loyalties are tenuous and difficult to maintain between men and women and parents and children, it is in fact because they are constrained by powerful political and economic conditions. These conditions can be altered only by activities directed toward changing political awareness and policies that would alter basic economic structures.

Political life in the imagery created by Gilder, the Friedmans, and others operates at the level of the relationships in the family and household, not in the world of multinational corporations and the power of the executive branch of governments. To perpetuate this atomized, microversion of the political order is most convenient to those who hold the more substantial resources and scope of decision-making power. Elites are free from challenge if people can be persuaded that little, if any, political or economic significance happens outside the orbit of the household. These assumptions reflect a long-standing belief among conservatives that nothing of lasting worth can be accomplished by the mass of people (certainly women) asserting their interests in opposition to elites, or that protest can win permanent improvements.

For all their celebration of the value of "freedom," the authors are not averse to placing women, children, and ordinary people in general under constraint. The word free is simply redefined to include "choice" in those very circumstances when limits to the range of options force people into behaviors and experiences they regard as inadequate and undesirable. People are in no real sense "free to choose" when the elimination of alternatives makes them endure hardships or accept exploitation.

The inability of the free-market authors to make use of social science research in a way consistent with the logical implications of this research is not accidental. They choose to ignore or misrepresent ideas, theories, and research that are inconsistent with their image of salvation by the rich and the traditional patriarchal family. The fact that these authors' works have been on best-seller lists for a long while is not surprising. Beliefs that prevent people from understanding the causes of their private troubles have great social utility. In a society dominated by inequality, modes of thought that distort the nature of social structure are more widespread and more highly regarded than critical studies based on scientific evidence that raise difficult questions about our quality of life.

The free-market viewpoints described here have an important social function: they break down the energies of dissent. They delay the rational public debate that is needed to form coherent political commitments and a more humane world built on caring and social responsibility for others. They create a pseudoversion of reality in which the myth of the traditional patriarchal family and micro-marketplace are as believable as anything else. Their arguments are accepted because the myths seem plausible and familiar, whereas the social research that contradicts the myths is complex and unfamiliar. It is little wonder that these viewpoints are as popular as they are with the more well-off segments of American society.

There are economic alternatives for women besides dependence on men, inadequate wages in work, or welfare that is set at levels below what is required for necessities. These alternatives require changes in basic institutions that are not gender specific; that is, they will benefit not only women, but all who are outside the privileged positions in our society. Although it is beyond the scope of this chapter to analyze a feminist economic program, it is possible to suggest some of its major features.

1. There must be meaningful jobs at adequate compensation and decent working conditions available for everyone willing and able to work.

2. There must be strong action to remove the barriers to full and equal employment for women and minorities.

3. There must be job training, child care, and medical care for all those who are unemployed, underemployed, or without the benefits in their jobs needed to support humane personal and family lives.

4. There must be a guaranteed minimum income to ensure that no one who is unemployed, caring for children, retired, sick, or disabled is poor.

5. There must be enhanced welfare services to support family living and assist individuals to escape poverty.

6. There must be citizen participation in the planning and decision-making processes that are concerned with public investment for human needs.

The assumption behind these proposals is that the right to subsistence is a human right that takes precedence over the satisfaction of selfish wants and private profits. These changes will almost certainly require public investment to organize the production of goods and delivery of services not now provided in the private profit economy. Also, a shorter standard work week would permit the creation of additional jobs and the expansion of employment. It will probably be necessary to shift the balance between military and domestic spending. The kinds of decisions and planning needed to serve the public good will require more widely distributed power and greater accountability of elites. There are a growing number of analyses that link planning and decentralized, democratic, political, and economic systems (Bluestone and Harrison; Bowles et al.; Carnoy and Shearer; Cohen and Rogers).

In the long run, changes that create more satisfying human lives and family well-being are social investments with the potential for much greater return than undirected spending for capital equipment. A society based on citizen participation in democratic planning to fulfill social goals has a worthier and more productive future than one designed around the private profits of the few. In any case, we cannot afford to perpetuate the economic irrationalities and social disruptions of the current economy without sacrificing the interest of those least able to protect themselves from their hazards.

Works Cited

Ackerman, Frank. *Reaganomics; Rhetoric vs. Reality.* Boston: South End, 1982.

Arrow, Kenneth. "Free to Choose." *New Republic* 22 (1980):25–28.

Bernard, Jessie. *The Female World.* New York: The Free Press, 1981.

Bluestone, Barry, and Bennett Harrison. *The Deindustrialization of America.* New York: Basic Books, 1982.

Bowles, Samuel, David M. Gordon, and Thomas E. Weisskopf. *Beyond the Waste Land: A Democratic Alternative to Economic Decline.* New York: Anchor Books, 1984.

Brody, David, *Workers in Industrial America.* New York: Oxford University Press, 1981.

Carnoy, Martin, and Derek Shearer. *Economic Democracy.* Armonk, NY: M. E. Sharpe, 1980.

Cohen, Joshua, and Joel Rogers. *On Democracy.* New York: Basic Books, 1977.

Edsall, Thomas Byrne. *The New Politics of Inequality.* New York: W. W. Norton, 1984.

Ehrenreich, Barbara. *The Hearts of Men.* New York: Anchor Books, 1984.

Friedman, Milton, and Rose Friedman. *Free to Choose.* New York: Harcourt Brace Jovanovich, 1980.

Garfinkel, Irwin, and Robert H. Haveman. *Earnings Capacity, Poverty, and Inequality.* New York: Academic Press, 1977.

Gilder, George. *Wealth and Poverty.* New York: Basic Books, 1981.

Heilbroner, Robert L. "The Road to Selfdom." *New York Review of Books* 17 (1980):3–8.

Jencks, Christopher, et al. *Inequality: A Reassessment of the Effect of Family and Schooling in America.* New York: Harper & Row, 1973.

Kemp, Jack. *An American Renaissance.* New York: Harper & Row, 1979.

Lekachman, Robert. *Greed Is Not Enough: Reaganomics.* New York: Pantheon, 1982.

Lynd, Robert S., and Helen Merrell Lynd. *Middletown in Transition.* New York: Harcourt, Brace & World, 1937.

Majka, Linda C. "The Impact of Recent Economic Change on Families and the Role of Women." In *The Changing Family,* edited by Stanley Saxton et al., 99–108. Chicago: Loyola University Press, 1984.

————. "Neoconservative Perspectives on Economic Inequalities Among Families." In *Families and Economic Distress,* edited by Patricia Voydanoff and Linda Majka. Beverly Hills, CA: Sage, 1988.

Montgomery, David. *Workers' Control in America.* New York: Cambridge University Press, 1980.

Osmond, Marie Withers. "Cross-Societal Family Research." *Journal of Marriage and the Family* 42 (1980):995–1016.

Pankhurst, Jerry G., and Sharon K. Houseknecht. "The Family, Politics, and Religion in the 1980s: In Fear of the New Individualism." *Journal of Family Issues* 4 (1983):5–34.

Pearce, Diana. "Women in Poverty." In *The American Promise: Equal Justice and Economic Opportunity,* edited by Arthur I. Blaustein, 7–31. New Brunswick, NJ: Transaction, 1982.

Pechman, Joseph A. *Who Paid the Taxes, 1966–85.* Washington, DC: Brookings Institution, 1985.

Piven, Frances Fox, and Richard A. Cloward. *The New Class War.* New York: Pantheon, 1982.

Ross, Heather L. "Poverty: Women and Children Last." In *Economic Independence for Women: The Foundation for Equal Rights,* edited by Jane Roberts Chapman, 137–54. Beverly Hills, CA: Sage, 1976.

————, and Isabel V. Sawhill. *Time of Transition: The Growth of Families Headed by Women*. Washington, DC: The Urban Institute, 1975.

Sarri, Rosemary C. "The Impact of Federal Policy Change on the Well-being of Poor Women and Children." In *Families and Economic Distress,* edited by Patricia Voydanoff and Linda Majka. Beverly Hills, CA: Sage, 1988.

Sawhill, Isabel. "Discrimination and Poverty Among Women Who Head Families." In *Women and the Workplace,* edited by Martha Blaxall and Barbara Reagan, 201–11. Chicago: University of Chicago Press, 1976.

Schlozman, Kay Lehman. "Women and Unemployment: Assessing the Biggest Myths." In *Women: A Feminist Perspective,* 2d ed., edited by Jo Freeman, 290–312. Palo Alto, CA: Mayfield, 1979.

Shortridge, Kathleen. "Poverty Is a Woman's Problem." In *Women: A Feminist Perspective,* 3d ed., edited by Jo Freeman, 492–501. Palo Alto, CA: Mayfield, 1984.

Thurow, Lester C. *The Zero-Sum Society.* New York: Basic Books, 1980.

Tyler, Gus. "The Friedman Inventions." *Dissent* 27 (1980): 279–90.

Wanniski, Jude. *The Way the World Works.* New York: Basic Books, 1978.

Winnick, Andrew J. "The Changing Distribution of Income and Wealth in the U.S.—1960–1985." In *Families and Economic Distress,* edited by Patricia Voydanoff and Linda Majka. Beverly Hills, CA: Sage, 1988.

Wrigley, Edward Anthony. *Population and History.* New York: McGraw-Hill, 1969.

————. "The Process of Modernization and the Industrial Revolution in England." *Journal of Interdisciplinary History* 3 (1972): 225–59.

CHAPTER 7

The Science Question in Feminism

SANDRA G. HARDING

SINCE THE MID-1970s feminist criticisms of science have evolved
from a reformist to a revolutionary position, from analyses that
offered the possibility of improving the science we have, to calls
for a transformation in the very foundations both of science and
of the cultures that accord it value. We began by asking, "What
is to be done about the situation of women in science?"—the
"woman's question" in science. Now feminists often pose a
different question: "Is it possible to use, for emancipatory ends,
sciences that are apparently so intimately involved in Western,
bourgeois, and masculine projects?"—the "science question" in
feminism.

Feminist scholars have studied women, men, and social relations between the genders within, across, and insistently against
the conceptual frameworks of the disciplines. In each area we
have come to understand that what we took to be humanly
inclusive problematics, concepts, theories, objective methodologies, and transcendental truths are in fact far less than that.
Instead, these products of thought bear the mark of their collective and individual creators, and the creators in turn have been
distinctively marked as to gender, class, race, and culture. We
can now discern the effects of these cultural markings in the
discrepancies between the methods of knowing and the interpretations of the world provided by the creators of modern Western
culture, and those characteristic of the rest of us. Western

Dr. Harding's lecture at the University of Dayton was based on her book *The
Science Question in Feminism*. Copyright © 1986 by Cornell University. The
material in this chapter is excerpted from the book and is used by permission of
the publisher, Cornell University Press.

culture's favored beliefs mirror in sometimes clear and sometimes distorting ways not the world as it is or as we might want it to be, but the social projects of their historically identifiable creators.

The natural sciences are a comparatively recent subject of feminist scrutiny. The critiques excite immense anticipation—or fear—yet they remain far more fragmented and less clearly conceptualized than feminist analyses in other disciplines.

To draw attention to the lack of a developed feminist theory for the critique of the natural sciences is not to overlook the contributions these young, but flourishing lines of inquiry have made. In a very short period of time we have derived a far clearer picture of the extent to which science, too, is gendered. Now we can begin to understand the economic, political, and psychological mechanisms that keep science sexist and that must be eliminated if the nature, uses, and valuations of knowledge-seeking are to become humanly inclusive ones. Each of these lines of inquiry raises intriguing political and conceptual issues, not only for the practices of science and the ways these practices are legitimated, but also for each other.

Equity Studies

First of all, equity studies have documented the massive historical resistance to women's getting the education, credentials, and jobs available to similarly talented men (Rossiter; Walsh); they have also identified the psychological and social mechanisms through which discrimination is informally maintained even when the formal barriers have been eliminated. [1] Motivation studies have shown why boys and men more often want to excel at science, engineering, and math than do girls and women (Aldrich). But should women want to become "just like men" in science, as many of these studies assume? That is, should feminism set such a low goal as mere equality with men? And to which men in science should women want to be equal—to underpaid and exploited lab technicians as well as Nobel prize winners?[2] Moreover, should women want to contribute to scientific projects that have sexist, racist, and classist problematics and outcomes? Should they want to be military researchers? Furthermore, what has been the effect of women's naiveté about the depth and extent of masculine resistance? That is, would women have struggled to enter science if they had understood how little equity would be produced by eliminating the formal barriers against women's participation (Rossiter)? Finally, does the increased presence of women in science have any effect at all on the nature of scientific problematics and outcomes?[3]

Uses and Abuses of Science

Second, studies of the uses and abuses of biology, the social sciences, and their technologies have revealed the ways science is used in the service of sexist, racist, homophobic, and classist social projects. Oppressive reproductive policies; white men's management of all women's domestic labor; the stigmatization of, discrimination against, and medical "cure" of homosexuals; gender discriminations in workplaces—all these have been justified on the basis of sexist research and maintained through technologies, developed out of this research, that move control of women's lives from women to men of the dominant group.[4] Despite the importance of these studies, critics of the sexist uses of science often make two problematic assumptions: that there is a value-free, pure scientific research which can be distinguished from the social uses of science, and that there are proper uses of science with which we can contrast its improper uses. Can we really make these distinctions? Is it possible to isolate a value-neutral core from the uses of science and its technologies? And what distinguishes improper from proper uses? Furthermore, each misuse and abuse has been racist and classist as well as oppressive to women. This becomes clear when we note that there are different reproductive policies, forms of domestic labor, and forms of workplace discrimination mandated for women of different classes and races even within U.S. culture at any single moment in history.[5] (Think, for instance, of the current attempt to restrict the availability of abortion and contraceptive information for some social groups at the same time that sterilization is forced on others. Think of the resuscitation of scientifically supported sentimental images of motherhood and nuclear forms of family life for some at the same time that social supports for mothers and nonnuclear families are systematically withdrawn for others.) Must not feminism take on as a central project of its own the struggle to eliminate class society and racism, homophobia and imperialism, in order to eliminate the sexist uses of science?[6]

Challenges to Pure Science

Third, in the critiques of biology and the social sciences, two kinds of challenges have been raised, not just to the actual, but to the possible existence of any pure science at all.[7] The selection and definition of problematics—deciding what phenomena in the world need explanation, and defining what is problematic about them—have clearly been skewed toward men's perception of what they find puzzling.[8] Surely it is "bad science" to assume that men's problems are everyone's problems, thereby leaving unexplained many things that women find problematic, and to assume that men's explanations of what they find problematic are undistorted by their gender needs and desires. But is this merely—or perhaps even—an example of bad science? Will not the selection and definition of problems always bear the social fingerprints of the dominant groups in a culture? With these questions we glimpse the fundamental value-ladenness of knowledge-seeking, and thus the impossibility of distinguishing between bad science and science-as-usual.[9] Furthermore, the design and interpretation of research again and again has proceeded in masculine-biased ways. But if problems are necessarily value-laden, if theories are constructed to explain problems, if methodologies are always theory-laden, and if observations are methodology-laden, can there be value-neutral design and interpretation of research? This line of reasoning leads us to ask whether it is possible that some kinds of value-laden research are nevertheless maximally objective. For example, are overtly antisexist research designs inherently more objective than overtly sexist or, more important, "sex-blind" (i.e., gender-blind) ones? And are antisexist inquiries that are also self-consciously antiracist more objective than those that are not? There are precedents in the history of science for preferring the distinction between objectivity-increasing and objectivity-decreasing social values to the distinction between value-free and value-laden research. A different problem is raised by asking what implications these criticisms of biology and social science have for areas such as physics and chemistry, where the subject matter purportedly is physical nature rather than social beings ("purportedly" because, as we shall see, we must be skeptical about being able to make any clear distinctions between the physical and the nonphysical). What implications could these findings and this kind of reasoning about objectivity have for our understanding the scientific world view more generally?

Metaphors of Gender Politics

Fourth, the related techniques of literary criticism, historical interpretation, and psychoanalysis have been used to "read science as a text" in order to reveal the social meanings—the hidden symbolic and structural agendas—of purportedly value-neutral claims and practices. [10] In textual criticism, metaphors of gender politics in the writings of the fathers of modern science, as well as in the claims made by the defenders of the scientific world view today, are no longer read as individual idiosyncrasies or as irrelevant to the meanings science has for its enthusiasts. [11] Furthermore, the concern to define and maintain a series of rigid dichotomies in science and epistemology no longer appears to be a reflection of the progressive character of scientific inquiry; rather, it is inextricably connected with specifically masculine—and perhaps uniquely Western and bourgeois—needs and desires. Objectivity versus subjectivity, the scientist as knowing subject versus the objects of his inquiry, reason versus the emotions, mind versus body—in each case the former has been associated with masculinity and the latter, with femininity. In each case it has been claimed that human progress requires the former to achieve domination of the latter. [12]

Valuable as these textual criticisms have been, they raise many questions. What relevance do the writings of the fathers of modern science have to contemporary scientific practice? What theory would justify regarding these metaphors as fundamental components of scientific explanations? How can metaphors of gender politics continue to shape the cognitive form and content of scientific theories and practices even when they are no longer overtly expressed? And can we imagine what a scientific mode of knowledge-seeking would look like that was not concerned to distinguish between objectivity and subjectivity, reason and the emotions?

Epistemological Questions

Fifth, a series of epistemological inquiries has laid the basis for an alternative understanding of how beliefs are grounded in social experiences, and of what kind of experience should ground the beliefs we honor as knowledge.[13] These feminist epistemologies[14] imply a relation between knowing and being, between epistemology and metaphysics, that is an alternative to the dominant epistemologies developed to justify science's modes of knowledge-seeking and ways of being in the world.

The radical feminist position holds that the epistemologies, metaphysics, ethics, and politics of the dominant forms of science are androcentric and mutually supportive; that despite the deeply ingrained Western cultural belief in science's intrinsic progressiveness, science today primarily serves regressive social tendencies; and that the social structure of science, many of its applications and technologies, its modes of defining research problems and designing experiments, its ways of constructing and conferring meanings are not only sexist, but also racist, classist, and culturally coercive. In their analyses of how gender symbolism, the social division of labor by gender, and the construction of individual gender identity have affected the history and philosophy of science, feminist thinkers have challenged the intellectual and social orders at their very foundations.

139

These feminist critiques, which debunk much of what we value in modern Western culture, appear to emerge from outside this culture. That is indeed the case insofar as women have been excluded from the processes of defining the culture and have been conceived as the "other" against which men in power define their projects. Yet such destabilizing, "exploding," of the categories of social practice and thought is firmly within the tradition of modern Western history and its explicit commitment to criticism of traditional social practices and beliefs. One such belief is that androcentrism is "natural" and right; another is faith in the progressiveness of scientific rationality. From this perspective the feminist critiques of science may be seen as calling for a more radical intellectual, moral, social, and political revolution than the founders of modern Western cultures could have imagined. Historically it is just such revolutions—and not the process of scientific inquiry alone—that have fostered the development of progressive kinds of knowledge-seeking.

It should not need to be said—but probably does—that I do not want to be understood as recommending that we throw out the baby with the bathwater. We do not imagine giving up speaking or writing just because our language is deeply androcentric; nor do we propose an end to theorizing about social life once we realize that thoroughly androcentric perspectives inform even our feminist revisions of social theories we inherit. Similarly I am not proposing that humankind would benefit from renouncing attempts to describe, explain, and understand the regularities, underlying causal tendencies, and meanings of the natural and social worlds just because the sciences we have are androcentric. I am seeking an end to androcentrism, not to systematic inquiry. But an end to androcentrism will require far-reaching transformations in the cultural meanings and practices of that inquiry.

When we first began theorizing our experiences during the second women's movement a mere decade and a half ago, we knew our task would be a difficult though exciting one. But I doubt that in our wildest dreams we ever imagined we would have to reinvent both science and theorizing itself in order to make sense of women's social experience.

Notes

In the course of her lecture, Dr. Harding elaborated on some of the themes in this chapter. The editors have freely paraphrased these elaborations where that might be helpful to the reader. Notes that contain such paraphrases are marked (Ed.). All other notes are Dr. Harding's.

1. (Ed.) In view of the claim that science is sex-blind, it is paradoxical that there has been such strong resistance to the entrance of women into science. Nevertheless, the history is one of stubborn resistance on the part of both European and American universities to the admission of women into their graduate programs (cf. Rossiter for details). In some cases, when the universities did finally admit women, they refused to grant them the doctorate, no matter how outstanding their work. Johns Hopkins Medical School only agreed to the admission of women students because a strong-minded donor, Mary Elizabeth Garrett, made that a condition of her grant. Christine Ladd-Franklin completed her work at Hopkins in 1882; she was awarded her Hopkins Ph.D. forty-four years later, after she achieved an international reputation as a psychologist. Although Radcliffe Graduate School began offering the doctorate in 1902, Harvard proper did not grant graduate degrees to women until 1963.

Sociological studies show that women in science today are discriminated against both horizontally and vertically; that is, they are to be found in some disciplines rather than in others (more in the "soft" than in the "hard" sciences) and at the lower echelons. In fact at one time there was a field called cosmetic chemistry, a kind of ghetto that women were encouraged to enter. This research also shows that women cannot develop the capital of prestige in the way their male colleagues do. The same research report will be rated higher by both women and men when it bears the name of John Smith rather than Joan Smith. Both women and men cite the work of men more than that of women. Ten years after graduation, with equal abilities and equally good degrees, the men will have advanced farther than the women on the academic ladder.

2. (Ed.) It simply is not true that there are few women in science. Women are in science in large numbers, but in the lower ranks. The lower one goes, the more women one will find. There are too few women directing the scientific enterprise, and a disproportionately large percentage at the lower levels as lab technicians, popularizers, textbook writers and editors, illustrators, and teachers in elementary and secondary schools.

3. (Ed.) The equity issue is the least threatening of the feminist

critiques, yet it is a radical challenge. If gender itself is an obstacle to women's gaining equity in science, then affirmative action issues are radical issues, requiring an immense degree of change in the larger society as well as in its scientific institutions.

4. See Ethel Tobach and Betty Rosoff, eds., *Genes and Gender,* vols., 1–4 (New York: Gordian Press, 1978, 1979, 1981, 1984); Brighton Women and Science Group, *Alice Through the Microscope* (London: Virago Press, 1980); Barbara Ehrenreich and Deirdre English, *For Her Own Good: 150 Years of Experts' Advice to Women* (New York: Doubleday, 1979); Joan Rothchild, *Machina ex Dea: Feminist Perspectives on Technology* (Elmsford, NY: Pergamon Press, 1983); Jan Zimmerman, ed., *The Technological Woman: Interfacing with Tomorrow* (New York: Praeger, 1983); Rita Arditti, Renate Duelli-Klein, and Shelly Minden, eds., *Test-Tube Women: What Future for Motherhood?* (Boston: Pandora Press, 1984).

5. (Ed.) For instance, contraceptive technologies were developed' on poor women in the Third World; some of the drugs that have been banned in the United States as unsafe have been dumped on Third World markets. Half the surgery done on women in the United States today is gynecological or obstetrical, much of it unnecessary. Some products dangerous to women's health (e.g., the Dalkon shield) have been marketed with inadequate research and without regard for consumer safety.

6. (Ed.) In her lecture, Dr. Harding raised these further questions: Are these merely abuses of science, or are they part of science's fundamental ethic? Is scientific domination of nature really about some people developing technologies to gain unequal access to natural resources that they use to dominate other people? Can a science so intimately involved with government and industry be innocent of the domination and profiteering characteristic of the agencies it relies on for funding?

7. The literature here is immense. For examples of these criticisms, see Helen Longino and Ruth Doell, "Body, Bias, and Behavior: A Comparative Analysis of Reasoning in Two Areas of Biological Science," *Signs* 9 (1983):206–27; Ruth Hubbard, M. S. Henifin, and Barbara Fried, eds., *Biological Woman: The Convenient Myth* (Cambridge, MA: Schenkman, 1982); Michael Gross and Mary Beth Averill, "Evolution and Patriarchal Myths of Scarcity and Competition," in *Discovering Reality: Feminist Perspectives on Epistemology, Metaphysics, Methodology and Philosophy of Science,* ed. S. Harding and M. Hintikka (Dordrecht: Reidel, 1983); Tobach and Rosoff, *Genes and Gender;* Marcia Millman and Rosabeth Moss Kanter, eds., *Another Voice: Feminist Perspectives on Social Life and Social Science* (New York: Anchor Books, 1975); Margaret Anderson, *Thinking About Women* (New

York: Macmillan, 1983); Marcia Westkott, "Feminist Criticism of the Social Sciences," *Harvard Educational Review* 49 (1979).

8. (Ed.) The selection of problems has been highly skewed to what the ruling groups find problematic. Thus there have been endless studies by psychiatrists that explain women's bizarre behavior, but not until the women's movement did women begin explaining the bizarre behavior of psychiatrists.

9. (Ed.) Thus there is bias in the design of research if all the researchers are male and they interview only male subjects about what women and men think or believe about some question. There is bias if the researchers (as was the case with McClelland and Kohlberg) discard the results from the female subjects.

10. Good examples are Evelyn Fox Keller, *Reflections on Gender and Science* (New Haven, CT: Yale University Press, 1984); Carolyn Merchant, *The Death of Nature: Women, Ecology and the Scientific Revolution* (New York: Harper & Row, 1980); Susan Griffin, *Woman and Nature: The Roaring Inside Her* (New York: Harper & Row, 1978); Jane Flax, "Political Philosophy and the Patriarchal Unconscious: A Psychoanalytic Perspective on Epistemology and Metaphysics," in Harding and Hintikka, eds., *Discovering Reality;* L. J. Jordanova, "Natural Facts: A Historical Perspective on Science and Sexuality," in *Nature, Culture and Gender,* ed., C. MacCormack and M. Strathern (New York: Cambridge University Press, 1980); Maurice Bloch and Jean Bloch, "Women and the Dialectics of Nature in the Eighteenth Century French Thought," in *Nature, Culture and Gender;* Sandra Harding, "The Norms of Social Inquiry and Masculine Experience," in *PSA 1980,* vol. 2, ed. P. D. Asquith and R. N. Giere (East Lansing, MI: Philosophy of Science Association, 1980).

11. (Ed.) Scientists and science enthusiasts have frequently called on a sexual rhetoric available to them that they use as a moral and political support for science, but it is a rhetoric that brings dishonor to women. Thus Machiavelli, writing about the usefulness of science for mastering the potential violence of fate, says, "Fortune is a woman and it is necessary if you wish to master her to conquer her by force." And Francis Bacon explains the experimental method in these words: "For you have but to hound nature in her wanderings and you will be able when you like to lead and drive her afterwards to the same place again. Neither ought a man to make scruple of entering and penetrating into those holes and corners when the inquisition of truth is his whole object." And a contemporary philosopher of science, Paul Feyerabend, recommends his own philosophy of science by saying: "Such a development . . . changes science from a stern and demanding mistress into an attractive and yielding courtesan who tries to anticipate every wish of her lover. Of course, it is up to us to choose

143

either a dragon or a pussy cat for our company. I think I do not have to explain my own preferences."

12. The key "object-relations" theorists among these textual critics are Dorothy Dinnerstein, *The Mermaid and the Minotaur: Sexual Arrangements and Human Malaise* (New York: Harper & Row, 1976); Nancy Chodorow, *The Reproduction of Mothering* (Berkeley: University of California Press, 1978); Flax, "Political Philosophy." See also Isaac Balbus, *Marxism and Domination* (Princeton, NJ: Princeton University Press, 1982).

13. See Flax, "Political Philosophy" Hilary Rose, "Hand, Brain and Heart: A Feminist Epistemology for the Natural Sciences," *Signs* 9 (1983):73–90; Nancy Hartsock, "The Feminist Standpoint: Developing the Ground for a Specifically Feminist Historical Materialism," in Harding and Hintikka, eds., *Discovering Reality* op. cit.; Dorothy Smith, "Women's Perspective as a Radical Critique of Sociology," *Sociological Inquiry* 44 (1974); Dorothy Smith, "Some Implications of a Sociology for Women," in *Woman in a Man-Made World: A Socioeconomic Handbook,* ed. N. Glazer and H. Waehrer (Chicago: Rand-McNally, 1977); Dorothy Smith, "A Sociology for Women," in *The Prism of Sex: Essays in the Sociology of Knowledge,* ed. J. Sherman and E. T. Beck (Madison: University of Wisconsin Press, 1979); Dorothy Smith, "The Experienced World as Problematic: A Feminist Method," Sorokin Lecture no. 12 (Saskatoon: University of Saskatchewan, 1981); Sandra Harding, "Why Has the Sex-Gender System Become Visible Only Now?" in Harding and Hintikka, eds., *Discovering Reality* Elizabeth Fee, "Women's Nature and Scientific Objectivity," in *Woman's Nature: Rationalizations of Inequality,* ed. M. Lowe and R. Hubbard (New York: Pergamon Press, 1981). Donna Haraway, "A Manifesto for Cyborgs: Science, Technology and Socialist Feminism in the 1980s," *Socialist Review* 80 (1985), proposes a somewhat different epistemology for feminism.

14. (Ed.) An epistemology is a theory of knowledge, a theory about the way we justify our beliefs. The epistemology that underlies contemporary science assumes a neutral, dispassionate observer. But feminist inquiries are politicized; that is, they are motivated by the desire to overcome the devaluation of women as persons, as thinkers, as contributors to society. How, then, can feminists claim that their politicized inquiries are more objective than the supposedly dispassionate inquiries of science? Feminist empiricists argue that feminist politics are a good thing for scientific research because they enable the sexist and androcentric blinders to be removed. Women scientists, and everyone who begins inquiry from the perspective of women's experience, are more likely to notice androcentric biases.

Works Cited

Aldrich, Michele L. "Women in Science." *Signs* 4 (1978):126–35.

Anderson, Margaret. *Thinking About Women.* New York: Macmillan, 1983.

Arditti, Rita, Renate Duelli-Klein, and Shelly Minden, eds. *Test-Tube Women: What Future for Motherhood?* Boston: Pandora Press, 1984.

Balbus, Isaac. *Marxism and Domination.* Princeton, NJ: Princeton University Press, 1982.

Bloch, Maurice, and Jean Bloch. "Women and the Dialectics of Nature in Eighteenth Century French Thought." In *Nature, Culture and Gender,* edited by C. MacCormack and M. Strathern. New York: Cambridge University Press, 1980.

Brighton Women and Science Group. *Alice Through the Microscope.* London: Virago Press, 1980.

Chodorow, Nancy, *The Reproduction of Mothering.* Berkeley: University of California Press, 1978.

Dinnerstein, Dorothy. *The Mermaid and the Minotaur: Sexual Arrangements and Human Malaise.* New York: Harper & Row, 1976.

Ehrenreich, Barbara, and Deirdre English. *For Her Own Good: 150 Years of Experts' Advice to Women.* New York: Doubleday, 1979.

Fee, Elizabeth. "Women's Nature and Scientific Objectivity." In *Woman's Nature: Rationalizations of Inequality,* edited by M. Lowe and R. Hubbard. Elmsford, NY: Pergamon Press, 1981.

Flax, Jane. "Political Philosophy and the Patriarchal Unconscious: A Psychoanalytic Perspective on Epistemology and Metaphysics." In *Discovering Reality: Feminist Perspectives on Epistemology, Metaphysics, Methodology and Philosophy of Science,* edited by S. Harding and M. Hintikka. Dordrecht: Reidel, 1983..

Griffin, Susan. *Woman and Nature: The Roaring Inside Her.* New York: Harper & Row, 1978.

Gross, Michael, and Mary Beth Averill. "Evolution and Patriarchal Myths of Scarcity and Competition." In *Discovering Reality: Feminist Perspectives on Epistemology, Metaphysics, Methodology and Philosophy of Science,* edited by S. Harding and M. Hintikka. Dordrecht: Reidel, 1983.

Haraway, Donna. "Animal Sociology and a Natural Economy of the Body Politic." *Signs* 4 (1978):21–36.

Harding, Sandra. "The Norms of Social Inquiry and Masculine Experience." In *PSA 1980,* vol. 2, edited by P. D. Asquith and R. N. Giere. East Lansing, MI: Philosophy of Science Association, 1980.

————."Why Has the Sex-Gender System Become Visible Only Now?" In *Discovering Reality: Feminist Perspectives on Epistemology,*

Metaphysics, Methodology and Philosophy of Science, edited by S. Harding and M. Hintikka. Dordrecht: Reidel, 1983.

Hartsock, Nancy. "The Feminist Standpoint: Developing the Ground for a Specifically Feminist Historical Materialism." In *Discovering Reality: Feminist Perspectives on Epistemology, Metaphysics, Methodology and Philosophy of Science,* edited by S. Harding and M. Hintikka. Dordrecht: Reidel, 1983.

Hubbard, Ruth, M. S. Henifin, and Barbara Fried, eds. *Biological Woman: The Convenient Myth.* Cambridge, MA: Schenkman, 1982.

Jordanova, L. J. "Natural Facts: A Historical Perspective on Science and Sexuality." In *Nature, Culture and Gender,* edited by C. MacCormack and M. Strathern. New York: Cambridge University Press, 1980.

Keller, Evelyn Fox. *Reflections on Gender and Science.* New Haven, CT: Yale University Press, 1984.

Longino, Helen, and Ruth Doell. "Body, Bias, and Behavior: A Comparative Analysis of Reasoning in Two Areas of Biological Science." *Signs* 9 (1983):206–27.

Merchant, Carolyn. *The Death of Nature: Women, Ecology and the Scientific Revolution.* New York: Harper & Row, 1980.

Millman, Marcia, and Rosabeth Moss Kanter, eds. *Another Voice: Feminist Perspectives on Social Life and Social Science.* New York: Anchor Books, 1975.

Rose, Hilary. "Hand, Brain and Heart: A Feminist Epistemology for the Natural Sciences." *Signs* 9 (1983):73–90.

Rossiter, Margaret. *Women Scientists in America: Struggles and Strategies to 1940.* Baltimore, MD: Johns Hopkins University Press, 1982.

Rothchild, Joan. *Machina ex Dea: Feminist Perspectives on Technology.* Elmsford, NY: Pergamon Press, 1983.

Smith, Dorothy. "The Experienced World as Problematic: A Feminist Method." Sorokin Lecture no. 12. Saskatoon: University of Saskatchewan, 1981.

———."A Sociology for Women." In *The Prism of Sex: Essays in the Sociology of Knowledge,* edited by J. Sherman and E. T. Beck. Madison: University of Wisconsin Press, 1979.

———."Some Implications of a Sociology for Women." In *Woman in a Man-Made World: A Socioeconomic Handbook,* edited by N. Glazer and H. Waehrer. Chicago: Rand-McNally, 1977.

———."Women's Perspective as a Radical Critique of Sociology." *Sociological Inquiry* 44 (1974).

Tobach, Ethel, and Betty Rosoff, eds. *Genes and Gender,* vols., 1–4. New York: Gordian Press, 1978, 1979, 1981, 1984.

Walsh, Mary Roth. *Doctor Wanted, No Women Need Apply: Sexual*

Barriers in the Medical Profession, 1835–1975. New Haven, CT: Yale University Press, 1977.

Westkott, Marcia. "Feminist Criticism of the Social Sciences." *Harvard Educational Review* 49 (1979).

Zimmerman, Jan, ed. *The Technological Woman: Interfacing with Tomorrow*. New York: Praeger, 1983.

CHAPTER 8

Sexism as Ideology and Social System
Can Christianity Be Liberated
from Patriarchy?

ROSEMARY RADFORD RUETHER

A Definition of Patriarchy

IN ORDER TO address the question, can Christianity be liberated
from patriarchy, one has first to define what patriarchy is and
what effects it has had on the Christian churches, both theologically and structurally. Patriarchy refers to a legal, social, and
economic system of society that validates and enforces the
domination of male heads of families over dependent persons in
the household. In classical patriarchal systems, such as are found
in Hebrew law or Roman law, these dependent persons included
wives, dependent children, and slaves, as well as various other
categories of dependents, such as clients. Various groups of
males are also subjugated people in patriarchal systems. However, women are subjugated in patriarchal societies in a more
total sense than either male children or male slaves. The former
could grow into becoming independent householders. The latter might be emancipated and become householders. Women,
first as daughters and then as wives and sometimes even as
widows, were generically defined as people who were dependent on the patriarch or the male head of the household in which
they lived.

Patriarchy is not to be understood as peculiarly "Jewish," nor
to be identified only with Old Testament patriarchy. As a social
system it is found in classic religious and social systems

throughout the world. Some people have imagined that the patriarchal order is the aboriginal order of human society, and hence is "natural" or inevitable. For example, in 1891 Edward A. Westermarck reasserted the patriarchal concept of the original family against the nineteenth-century concept of J.J. Bachofen and others who had speculated that matriarchy preceded patriarchy. But anthropological scholarship over the past century and a half has modified this assumption. It appears that patriarchal social systems arose with the first developments of large private landholding, the change from gardening to plow agriculture, urbanization and class-stratified societies, including slavery, in about the beginning of the second millennium B.C. Before that, and alongside these patriarchal cultures, for hundreds of thousands of years, the predominant human patterns of hunting-gathering and hunting-gardening societies allowed for more equal gender relations, characterized by communal landholding, little or no class structure, and balanced spheres of production and power for adult men and women (Martin and Voorhes).

Ancient tribal societies that are more strictly patriarchal seem to have been those that lacked the female gathering and gardening role, such as nomadic animal-herding societies. It is notable that strictly patriarchal religions seem to have originated with the incursions of nomadic animal-herding tribes into settled agricultural areas, conquering the mother-right cultures that had developed there and co-opting or suppressing the religions with prominent mother goddesses into religions with a dominant or exclusively male god. This is particularly true of the two major patriarchal religions of Judaism and Islam. It is secondarily true of Christianity, which inherited a double patriarchal culture through both Judaism and Greco-Roman society and philosophy, but also inherited partially suppressed female symbols for deity as well (Ruether, *Sexism and God-Talk* 54–61).

The Status of Women Under Patriarchy

The status of women under patriarchy contains many nuances, depending on whether remnants of mother-right remain in the

149

society. In addition, economic and legal changes and the spread of education can create periods of liberalization of patriarchal law, as took place in the Hellenistic and, later, Roman periods. So it is difficult to define a single system that would be true of all patriarchal societies at all times. However, it is possible to generalize about the characteristics usually found in patriarchal societies, although not all may be found there in the same way and at the same time (Pomeroy 120–48).

First, women are legally defined as dependents of the male heads of their families: their fathers, husbands, or guardians. This means that women lack autonomous civil status or can exercise it only in extraordinary circumstances or through a male guardian. This means that women cannot exercise legal or political power in their own right. They cannot vote, hold office, represent themselves at law, or enter into contracts in their own name.

Second, women are economically dependent. This does not mean that women do not do productive labor, but that their economic productivity, whether in the home or out of the home, belongs to their fathers or husbands. Restrictions are placed on women as inheritors of property. Often, the property they can inherit or the dowries given them in marriage are managed by their husbands or other male relatives.

Women also suffer various restrictions of rights to their persons. This may mean that they cannot decide whom they will marry. This decision is made by the family, and they must comply. On marrying they leave membership in their own families and are adopted into the families of their husbands, often with exchange of goods between the two male heads of family. Because inheritance is through the father, female chastity before and during marriage is strictly guarded and violations severely punished in order to assure that the wife's child will be that of her husband. By contrast, males are sexually free and allowed access to a variety of second-class women, female servants, prostitutes, and concubines. Male children are preferred to female, and there is a sharp distinction between legitimate and illegitimate children.

Husbands were generally given the right physically to beat their wives, as well as children and slaves, although provision was usually made that husbands should not permanently injure or kill their wives. American law until the late nineteenth century still allowed husbands to beat their wives so long as they did not use a stick thicker than their thumb, hence the phrase "rule of thumb" (Steinmetz 89). The husband was regarded as having unlimited sexual access to his wife, whether she desired it or not, hence the difficulty even today of a wife making a legal charge of rape against her husband. Children were seen as legally belonging to the father, who also had the right to expose them or sell them into slavery, fates that fell disproportionately on unwanted female children.

The wife is seen as having no right to interfere in the generative effects of the male sexual act on her body, either by contraception or by abortion. Knowledge of contraception and abortion once was kept from wives, although such knowledge might exist and be practiced by prostitutes. The married woman's body and its "fruits" were seen as the private property of her husband. Rape also is viewed as an offense against the property rights of the father or husband. Rape of a "loose" woman (i.e., servant or prostitute) is not viewed as an offense in the same way as the rape of a married woman or a marriageable daughter. Patriarchal law also gives the male, but not the female, the right to divorce, particularly if the wife is adulterous or fails to produce a male heir.

Women are excluded from the exercise of public roles of power and culture and from the credentials that lead to these roles. This means that women cannot hold political or military leadership, although there may be exceptions to this law when women come into hereditary offices through lack of a male heir. Women are also generally excluded from priesthoods, especially those of the civil religion, and from professional roles that require higher education, such as lawyers, rhetoricians, and academically trained doctors. In general, women are excluded from higher education and from roles generated by education, such as scribes and teachers. This means that women are excluded both from access to learning and from forming public culture. This accounts for the almost exclusively male formation of public culture under patriarchy and the definition of women in the culture solely from the male point of view. Women typically have great difficulty gaining visibility, even when they manage to gain an education and produce cultural creations. Because the cultural creations of women are not incorporated into the public culture taught to the next generation of male students, women's cultural accomplishments are continually lost and erased from the collective cultural memory.

The Impact of the Patriarchal Model on Christianity

Patriarchal social systems with these characteristics form the predominant background of Western civilization, in both its Hebrew and its Greco-Roman roots. Patristic Christianity reverted to some of the more strict aspects of patriarchal society, negating some of the gains for women that had been won in late Roman society. Christianity modified patriarchy somewhat with the institution of female celibacy, which could counteract the marriage rights of fathers over daughters. It almost supported female consent to marriage and a single standard of sexual morality for men as well as women, combating concubinage, polygamy, and divorce, although medieval Christianity accepted prostitution as a necessary evil, following the opinion of Augustine in this matter.[1] On matters of female consent to marriage and on divorce, however, the church, in practice, often accommodated the dynastic needs of powerful feudal families (Herlihy ch. 1; Duby).

The European legal codes that emerged as national law in France, England, and Spain in the early modern period reflect a strengthening of patriarchal principles, annulling some of the access to education, guild membership, and political roles that had been enjoyed by some women in feudal and early urban society. In English and American society, and even longer in French society, such patriarchal law codes remained substantially intact until the twentieth century. It was only in the mid-nineteenth century that English and American women began to challenge this traditional legal structure that denied women higher education, civil rights, and property rights. It took approximately another eighty years for women to win the vote, most property rights, access to universities and professional education, and the right to enter the professions (i.e., doctors and lawyers) (Flexner). Access to the ordained clergy has been even slower to open to women, and except for token groups in the latter half of the nineteenth century, there has been major change in this area only in the past twenty-five years.

What this means is that Christianity, and Judaism before it, has modeled itself as an institution primarily after the patriarchal social system. The clergy has been seen as an ecclesiastical counterpart to the power of the father in the family, while the laity has been seen in the role of dependent wives and children. Women have been excluded both from the ordained clergy and from access to higher theological education and from the teaching of theology. Even lay leadership in the church, such as vestrymen or delegates to synods, has until recently been restricted to males. The church has not only modeled itself after the patriarchal social hierarchy, but has also acted as the ultimate ideological sanction for this system, naming it both in its ecclesiastical and its social forms as expressions of the will of God and the order of creation. Those few women who did manage to gain higher theological culture, either as nuns or, later through private libraries, either had to conform strictly to patriarchal limits on their ideas and activities or were vilified and persecuted as heretics.

This means that what we know about Christian women, their activities and ideas, until recently, is the product of patriarchal censorship. Women's ideas were censored, both in their lifetimes and after their deaths, to make them conform to male theological and social definitions of good women. And women themselves, in order to win approval and avoid punishment, conformed their own lives and ideas to this standard. Those few dissenting women whose names are known to us are remembered only through the screen of negative labels, and their writings were generally destroyed. Only occasionally have such dissenting women's writings escaped some of this censorship by accident, such as the preservation of the book of Marguerite Porete, *The Mirror of Simple Souls,* who was condemned and burned in 1310. But some copies of her book survived and were preserved in the writings of fourteenth-century monastic mysticism by being wrongly ascribed to a male writer (Shahar 54, 64).

This exclusion of critical voices drawn from women's experience (and the assimilation of the church into the role of religious sanctification of patriarchal society) has meant that the church's own theology and religious culture has been characterized by a pervasive androcentrism, supplemented by overt misogyny. By androcentrism one means the pervasive and unquestioned assumption that the male is the normative representative of humanity and the sole subject of culture. In speaking about the nature of "man," therefore, women are typically ignored altogether. They remain invisible and unnoticed. Or, when they are noticed and mentioned, they are defined solely in relation to the male, their differences from males being regarded as defects and their role that of subordinate and auxiliary to the male in limited roles having primarily to do with marriage and motherhood.

Overt hostility, or misogyny, toward women occurs in the tradition primarily when women are perceived as trying to break out of these limited roles and attempting to speak in their own right. It is in this context that women's nature is defined as both defective, in the sense of being incapable of autonomous existence, education, and leadership, and prone to evil. Such definitions have the effect of reinforcing women's silence and subordination as punishment for the sin of "getting out of their place." Because these negative definitions of women survive in the tradition, while the memory of women's dissent is erased, misogynist definitions are received in the tradition as a normative consensus of the past, without recognition of the conflicts over women's status that occasioned such statements. Thus, for example, the dictum that occurs in 1 Timothy 2:11–15:

> Let a woman learn in silence with all submissiveness. I permit no woman to teach or to have authority over men; she is to keep silent. For Adam was formed first, then Eve; and Adam was not deceived, but the woman was deceived and became a transgressor. Yet the woman will be saved through bearing children.

was occasioned by a strong countercultural tradition in first- and second-century Christianity that gave women roles in teaching, preaching, and evangelism, and that held out a vision of spiritual equality between men and women who had forsaken marriage and sexual relationships. 1 Timothy was written to combat this ascetic, egalitarian tradition, which, in the first and second centuries, also claimed the authority of Paul, as in, for example, the *Acts of Paul and Thecla,* in which Thecla rejects marriage and is commissioned to preach by Paul.

But because the memory of this countercultural Christianity was repressed in the tradition, excluded from the canon, the statement of 1 Timothy was passed on in the tradition as the teaching of Paul and the consensus of the early church. This combination of misogyny and androcentrism, plus the erasure of dissenting female voices from the tradition, has had a pervasive influence on the shape of Christian theology and symbolism. We can summarize this pattern of Christian theology under the five categories of (1) anthropology, (2) doctrine of sin and salvation, (3) God-language, (4) Christology, and (5) ministry and the nature of the church.

In anthropology the male is defined as the normative human person. In the Genesis 2 account the male is seen as created first, with the female taken from his rib, a myth that reverses the actual relation of males to females in birth. This myth functions to locate the male as the primary expression of humanity and the female as secondary and auxiliary to the male. The Genesis 1 account, which defines humanity as made in the image of God, male and female, has been read in modern times as an egalitarian text. But it was not so read in the Christian tradition and was probably not intended to be egalitarian by its ancient Hebrew author. Rather, its author probably understood "man" or Adam, collectively, to be represented by the male. In the Christian tradition this was understood to mean that the male possessed the image of God, which was interpreted as the possession of rationality and authority. The woman was not made in the image of God except, as St. Augustine puts it, "when she is taken together with her husband who is her head" (*de Trinitate* 7.7.10). In herself the woman is seen as representing the body, and hence the subjugated part of the self.

The Christian doctrines of sin and salvation reinforce, with overt misogyny, the androcentrism inherent in these definitions of humanity. In Genesis 3 the woman is said to have initiated the sin of disobedience to God, which caused the expulsion of the primal human pair from paradise. This story, which is not accorded other mention in the rest of Hebrew scriptures, seems to have taken on new authority in Judaism during the Hellenistic era. The first reference to this theme in Genesis 3 is in the apocryphal work *Ecclesiasticus or the Wisdom of Ben Sirach,* 25:33, written about 180 B.C. This story was picked up and used in the 1 Timothy text mentioned earlier as the key proof text not only for woman's secondary, but also her punished status in society and the church. Woman is defined as having sinned in the beginning by getting out of her secondary and auxiliary relation to the male by taking initiative in questioning God's orders and acting contrary to God's will. Pain in childbirth and subjugation to her husband's will is thus defined as an expression of her punishment for this primal sin that lost to humanity original blessedness and imposed the troubles of harsh toil in an un-friendly world.

Woman is to be redeemed, according to such theological thought, by voluntary submission to her sexual role, the defini-tion of her nature through childbearing, and social subordina-tion to the male. Because women are to accept these roles, not only as their nature, but also as punishment for the primal sin that imposed all troubles on humanity, their guilt is limitless. In effect, any male physical and social abuse directed at her is to be accepted as her just deserts. If a male rapes her, she has caused it by being sexually provocative. If her husband beats her, she deserves it because she was insufficiently docile and submissive. The Christian scapegoating myth of the Fall becomes a per-vasive victim-blaming ideology toward women, which justifies any amount of male use and abuse of women and directs women silently to accept this treatment as their means of salva-tion.

God-language and Christology provide the divine counter-parts to androcentric anthropology. Although God is defined as a Spirit who is beyond human words and metaphors, neverthe-less, "He" is to be described as a male with male metaphors and social roles. Because males, but not females, represent the image of God, possessing reason and sovereignty, only male meta-phors are seen as appropriate for God. This further denies that women are theomorphic or possess the image of God, since female images or female persons cannot represent God.

Maleness, likewise, is seen as characterizing the divine Word or "Son" of God manifest in Christ. The maleness of the historical Jesus is thus seen as doubly necessary, both because it represents the maleness of God and the maleness of the Word or Son of God, and because only the human male possesses normative or complete humanity. This was reinforced in medieval theology by the appropriation of the false biology of Aristotle, which defined women as "misbegotten males" who possess a defective humanity, lacking in equal capacity for physical strength, intelligence, or moral self-control. Women, therefore, are not only not theomorphic, they are also not Christomorphic. They are redeemed by Christ, but they cannot image Christ or represent Christ.

This doctrine of Christ finds expression in the theology of ministry in the denial of ordained ministry to women on the grounds that they cannot image or represent Christ, or, as the *Vatican Declaration Against Women's Ordination* of 1976 puts it, "there must be a natural resemblance between the priest and Christ" (*Declaration* 37). The hierarchy of male over female in ministry is further accentuated by the patriarchal marriage symbolism in which God and Christ are imaged as a husband or bridegroom and the church, as the bride or wife. This metaphor is not based on companionate marriage, but on the assumption of a marriage relationship based on domination and submission. Similarly God or Christ is imaged as the head of the church, while the church is imaged as the body. Thus women become the symbols of creaturely and bodily existence that are to be ruled over, while the male, particularly as clergy, symbolizes the sovereignty of God and Christ that rules over creation and the church, or reason that rules over the body. Needless to say, this lends itself to a paternalistic definition of ministry in which the ordained clergy monopolize learning, teaching, preaching, and sacramental and administrative power, and the laity are variously defined as children or "sheep" who "pray, pay and obey."

Contesting Patriarchy: The Egalitarian Tradition

Given this pervasive history of patriarchal shaping of Christianity, both structurally and culturally, what hope can there possibly be for the liberation of Christianity from patriarchy? Why, one might ask, would anyone even want to bother? Such a judgment would be just if this dominant patriarchal tradition was the sole Christian tradition, and if there were not significant countercultural trends in both the Bible and the Christian tradition of theology and practice that provide alternatives. These alternatives have been joined in modern times by liberal and liberationist traditions, themselves rooted in Christian tradition, that have significantly transformed women's role in many Christian churches. Thus the churches today, particularly in the United States, demonstrate the features, not of univocal patriarchalism, but of a sharp conflict between liberalizing trends that promote the equality of women in society and in the church, and reactionary efforts to shore up patriarchal tradition. It is in this context of a contested patriarchal tradition that it is at least meaningful to ask how these two trends can continue to coexist in the Christian body and which of the two may eventually predominate.

What are the roots of this alternative egalitarian tradition? Basically, it is rooted in the prophetic tradition of Hebrew faith that sees God as located, not on the side of the wealthy and powerful in society, but on the side of the poor, the victimized people in society. This message was picked up and renewed by the Jesus movement within Judaism, with its message of God's favor on the poor and its criticism of the oppressive power of the temple priesthood and the scribal class. The dissenting trend was universalized in first-generation Christianity into a vision of a new humanity in which divisions of Jew and Greek, slave and free, male and female have been overcome in Christ (Ruether, *Sexism and God-Talk* 27–31).

However, so pervasive was the assumption of the patriarchal order as the natural or created order that early Christians could not imagine this new humanity of spiritual equality except in some new form of existence that would depart from marriage and procreation, and hence from the patriarchal family. It is in this eschatological or antifamilial form that Christian spiritual egalitarianism is picked up and perpetuated in Christian tradition, in a radical form by groups such as gnostics and Montanists, who were repressed as heretics, and in a modified form, in female monasticism. Moreover, spiritual egalitarianism continued to pop up again and again in popular renewal movements throughout the Middle Ages, such as the Waldensians in the twelfth century, and to appear again in the left wing of the Reformation among radical Puritans in the English Reformation. Quakers, or the Society of Friends, become the most consistent exponents of the theology of woman's spiritual equality and the implications of this for women's right to preach and minister in the church in the seventeenth century.

The seventeenth-century English setting generally provided the context for a host of dissenting and leveling movements that are the seed bed of the earliest feminism. Demands for an enlarged role for women in education and in church and political activities are heard from numerous female as well as some male tractarians in that period, from both the upper and the popular classes.

From these first English stirrings there flowed a variety of liberal and liberationist movements in the eighteenth and nineteenth centuries that challenged patriarchal order in terms of class hierarchy, slavery, and the subordination of women. Christian spiritual egalitarianism was expressed in secular form in the liberal ideology that declared that all human beings were created equal in the order of nature, all possessing the essential human qualities of rationality and moral conscience. From this common human nature there flow common human rights, according to liberal ideology. All social systems that institutionalize legal and social privileges based on inherited status are said to be inherently contrary to the true nature of things, and thus contrary to the will of God. Although this egalitarianism was originally applied only to bourgeois males in their contest with the old aristocracy, other groups, including women, were not slow to pick up on the implied universalism of this doctrine of human nature and to apply it to themselves.

In early nineteenth-century America this egalitarian anthropology was the foundational presupposition of a new revolutionary society, although it was still not applied to the civil rights of women, slaves, Indians, or propertyless white males. The first feminist movement in America came from such women as Sara and Angelina Grimké, Lucretia Mott, and Susan

B. Anthony, who had inherited the spiritual egalitarianism of the Quaker tradition and married it to liberal anthropology. These women could then reappropriate the liberal tradition into their interpretation of Christian faith and could claim that it was the Bible itself that taught that men and women were spiritually equal. Both women and men were created in the image of God and were equally endowed with reason, moral conscience, and authority over creation. Societies that denied women this equal human status and social role thus contravened the order of creation and the will of God (Schneir 35–48).

These women sought to reform, not only social and political institutions, but the church as well. In 1848, at the first Women's Rights Convention at Seneca Falls, New York, which claimed the egalitarian traditions of the American Declaration of Independence for women, the "Declaration of Sentiments and Resolutions" was written, which ends with a ringing claim to the ordained ministry.

> *Resolved:* That the speedy success of our cause depends upon the zealous and untiring efforts of both men and women for the overthrow of the monopoly of the pulpit, and for the securing to women an equal participation with men in the various trades, professions and commerce. (Quoted in Schneir 82)

Women in 1848 had already begun to be admitted to Oberlin College's theological curriculum, and in 1853 a graduate of this program, Antoinette Brown, became the first women to be ordained to the Christian ministry in the Congregational tradition. The nineteenth century saw several other small denominations—Methodist Protestants, Unitarians, and Universalists, and some others—open the ordained ministry to women. By the 1870s a few women were found in a variety of theological seminaries, mostly of the Unitarian, Methodist, and Congregationalist traditions. But mainstream Methodism, along with Lutherans and Presbyterians, rejected the ordination of women in the 1880s and diverted the energies of these first graduates of theological schools into the restored female diaconate and the foreign missionary fields.

This negative decision was not reversed until 1956, when the United Methodist Church and the northern Presbyterian

Church voted to ordain women. At the same time the Lutheran Churches of Denmark, Sweden, and Norway also accepted the ordination of women. From 1956 until the present there has been a steady increase of Protestant churches ordaining women, and those remaining Protestant churches, as well as the Anglican, Roman Catholic, and Eastern Orthodox Churches, have experienced rising dissent against their traditions of exclusion of women from ordination among their scholars and vocal women leaders (Zikmund, "Struggle" 193–241; "Winning" 339–83).

Although the numbers of women in theological seminaries remained small until the late 1960s, since then, in the United States as well as in other countries whose churches ordain women, such as Scandinavia and Holland, there has been a steady rise of the number of women in seminaries, until it has passed the 50 percent mark in some liberal seminaries and averages about a quarter of the total seminary population in the USA. Increasing numbers of women are also earning doctorates in theological studies and taking their place on seminary faculties. This means that the tradition of patriarchy is now under decisive challenge in the theological curriculum. Biblical studies, church history, theology, and ethics, as well as the applied disciplines, all are places in which pervasive traditions of androcentrism and misogyny are being challenged and alternative traditions are being rediscovered and developed. Feminist scholars, mostly female, but including some males as well, are beginning to envision a reconstruction of the Christian interpretations of God, Christ, human anthropology, sin and grace and church ministry, not only freed from overt patriarchy, but decisively aligned with the liberation of the church from patriarchy.

The Contemporary Conflict

This movement is not progressing without conflict. Some male students express their hostility to inclusive language and to attention to feminist questions in the curriculum. Women, although close to equal numbers in some seminary student bodies, are still only 6 percent of the ordained and employed clergy. Many local Christian churches are even more hostile to

161

women clergy and to inclusive language and symbols. When the *Inclusive Language Lectionary,* mandated by the National Council of Churches for most of mainline Protestantism, was released several years ago, many churches declared their refusal to use it. The members of the lectionary committee received a spate of hate mail and even threats on their lives. The politicized fundamentalist movement in the Christian churches seeks to reestablish the dogma of the subordination of women as the order of creation as the base for an assault on liberal and feminist gains in society. The defeat of the Equal Rights Amendment (ERA) and the continued assault on reproductive rights represent part of an effort to reestablish the patriarchal norm of family and culture. These attitudes are increasingly inserted into state and federal legislatures. The new chief justice of the U.S. Supreme Court, William Rehnquist, opposed the ERA in a legal memo to the President during the Nixon administration on the grounds that it threatened the patriarchal order of the family and of society. Thus today, as in the past, the conflict in the churches over women's place in theology and ministry is by no means isolated in the religious sphere, but is the religious ideological expression of a general cultural and social conflict between patriarchal and equalitarian views of the social order.

Liberal churchmen seek to satisfy the demands of women for equality with token accommodation to women in ministry in the lower ranks, but without probing the depths of the patriarchal bias in the Christian tradition. Part of this bias lies in lingering infallibilism in Christian ideology, which cannot admit to serious and sinful error in scripture and Christian tradition. As conflict with right-wing reactionary, patriarchal Christians heightens, this tokenism from liberal churchmen is likely to increase. They may try to limit further advance of women in ministry or deeper exploration of sexism in church tradition in the name of peace and reconciliation in the church. Women will become the scapegoats of discord in the churches.

As the more critical feminists in the churches see this limitation of liberal openness to women, more and more they will turn to alternative feminist groups as places for theological education and worship. These alternative structures, evident in the Women's Theological Center in Boston and the Women's

Alliance for Theology, Ethics and Ritual in Washington, D.C., as well as in the women-church movement in Catholicism (Ruether, *Women-Church*), are not being pursued over against the continuing effort to reform the churches, but to supplement these efforts and to provide an alternative, liberated structure within which to explore in greater depth the vision of a religious faith liberated from patriarchy. Women seek to experience a faith community whose mission is the redemption of humanity from patriarchy.

The outcome of this conflict is unclear, but what is indisputable is that Christianity, for the first time in its history, is faced with a large-scale challenge to the patriarchal interpretation of religion and an increasingly coherent vision of an alternative way of constructing the tradition from its very roots. The question for the future is perhaps not so much whether this alternative will prevail, as whether it will survive and continue to be a public option for the next generation of Christians, or whether its very existence will again be erased from the public memory of the churches, only to have to be reinvented and rediscovered again by a future generation of women.

Note

1. Augustine, *de Ordine*, PL xxxii, col. 1000: see Shulamith Shahar, *The Fourth Estate: A History of Women in the Middle Ages* (New York: Methuen, 1983), 106.

Works Cited

Augustine. *de Trinitate*. 7.7.10.
Bachofen, J. J. *Das Mutterrecht*. Stuttgart: Krais and Hoffman, 1861.
Declaration on the Question of the Admission of Women to the Ministerial Priesthood, 15 October 1976:5, 27.
Duby, George. *The Knight, the Lady and the Priest: The Making of Modern Marriage in Medieval France*. New York: Pantheon, 1983.
Flexner, Eleanor. *Century of Struggle: The Women's Rights Movement in the United States*. New York: Athenaeum, 1977.

Herlihy, David. *Medieval Households*. Cambridge, MA: Harvard University Press, 1985.

Martin, M. Kay, and Barbara Voorhes. *The Female of the Species*. New York: Columbia University Press, 1975.

Pomeroy, Sarah. *Goddesses, Whores, Wives and Slaves: Women in Classical Antiquity*. New York: Schocken, 1975.

Ruether, Rosemary. *Sexism and God-Talk: Towards a Feminist Theology*. Boston: Beacon Press, 1983.

————. *Women-Church: Theology and Practice of Feminist Liturgical Communities*. San Francisco: Harper & Row, 1985.

Schneir, Miriam, ed. *Feminism: Essential Historical Writings*. New York: Vintage, 1972.

Shahar, Shulamith. *The Fourth Estate: A History of Women in the Middle Ages*. New York: Methuen, 1983.

Steinmetz, Suzanne K. *Violence in the Family*. New York: Dodd & Mead, 1975.

Westermarck, Edward A. *The History of Human Marriage*. London: Macmillan, 1891.

Zikmund, Barbara Brown. "The Struggle for the Right to Preach." In *Women and Religion in America: The Nineteenth Century*, edited by Rosemary Ruether and Rosemary Keller, 193–241. New York: Harper & Row, 1983.

————. "Winning Ordination for Women in Mainstream Protestantism." In *Women and Religion in America: 1900–1968*, edited by Rosemary Ruether and Rosemary Keller, 339–83. New York: Harper & Row, 1986.

CHAPTER 9

Possibilities and Promise for Seeing Beyond Gender

PATRICIA ALTENBERND JOHNSON & JANET KALVEN

A Hermeneutic of Transformation

WHEN WE OPEN BOTH of our eyes, and when we train them to work together, we not only see more clearly, but we see with a depth of perception inaccessible to one eye alone. The opening of the feminist eye and the cooperative training of male and female seeing enable us to envision ourselves more fully, more humanly. The authors who have contributed to this book exemplify the clearer vision that is possible. They help us to envision the possibilities and the promise of this more complete vision. We will conclude by describing some of these possibilities and promises. We will look first at the Academy. This is of importance to us because it is where we work. But it is also important because it is where we educate those who will help envision the future: their own, humanity's, and the planet's. Possibilities and promises are not limited to the Academy. Indeed, outside the Academy the possibilities of human vision are often more fully exercised. And so we will conclude with a brief sketch of some of these emerging visions.

Our examination of the promises and possibilities that are created by the development of female vision within and outside the Academy will follow the four-step process that has emerged in the separate disciplines. In each discipline, as in history, the example in our first chapter, women have gained entry to the field, have worked to become accepted scholars, have begun to raise their own questions, have seen how those questions require a development apart from the traditional approach of the discipline, and then have recognized that this new approach offers challenges to the discipline that call for its change or transformation.

In the area of biblical theology this process has been called a hermeneutic of suspicion. Paul Ricoeur explains that this hermeneutic begins with the recognition that much which enters into and even gives focus to our understanding is unconscious. He identifies Freud as a prime example of someone who stresses the importance of a hermeneutic of suspicion. In the tradition of Freud, such a hermeneutic is suspicious of the claims we make for and about ourselves. We must constantly ask what has helped to form our understanding but remains unconscious and concealed.

Liberation theologians such as Juan Segundo and feminist theologians such as Elisabeth Schüssler Fiorenza also use what they call a hermeneutic of suspicion. They suggest that the understandings, in this case of the Bible, that develop in a culture are primarily formed by the experiences of those people and groups who have power. Such interpretations legitimate and perpetuate the existing power structures. Both Segundo and Fiorenza suggest that a hermeneutic of suspicion begins in the experience of those who are oppressed or dominated by the existing power structures. These people's experiences do not fit well into the prevailing understanding, and eventually this leads them to question the existing theory or interpretation. This initial questioning grows until the basic tenets and concepts that are central to the dominant understanding are also called into question. People who are engaged in the hermeneutic of suspicion begin to suggest new understandings that arise out of their experiences. These understandings critique and challenge the prevailing understandings.

The process that we will follow here begins with such a hermeneutic of suspicion, but in its full development it may more properly be called a *hermeneutic of transformation*. Women begin from their experiences to be suspicious of the theories and methods that dominate their fields and the Academy. In following out their suspicions they have begun to develop not only particular changes in a variety of areas, but also a transformation of human understanding, both theoretical and practical. The opening of the feminist eye begins a process of development in which (a) women enter and become skilled in fields or areas from which they have previously been excluded; (b) women reflect on these areas or disciplines from their own experiences, raise questions, and begin to do work that is influenced by their own experiences; (c) this work leads women to ask for and begin to make specific changes within the traditional framework or approach of the area or discipline; and (d) women recognize the inadequacy of these changes and begin working for transformation not only of the discipline or area, but also of the Academy and of the possibilities it provides for people.

Women's Studies as Impetus for Transformation

This process is clearly demonstrated in American higher education. In order to gain entry into the Academy, women had first to gain the requisite credentials. In 1950 only 10 percent of doctorates were awarded to women (Graham 766). This figure remained constant through the 1960s; by 1970 it began to climb two to three percentage points each year, until today women receive about 30 percent of the doctoral degrees. As women began to gain credentials, they also began to enter the Academy as full-time faculty. Although women are still underrepresented on faculties, especially at more prestigious institutions, their numbers have increased. And although women are still tenured at a lower rate than men (47 percent versus 69 percent), many women have gone through tenure review procedures and now are entering the upper faculty ranks (Owens). They have proved themselves as scholars and have entered into that period of an academic career in which a thinker, male or female, is freer to pursue her or his own concerns and interests. Many women have discovered that their questions and concerns have arisen out of their experiences as women or have focused on concerns that are of particular importance to women. Scholarship on, by, about, and for women has produced an immense body of new work in many areas. Much of this work not only looks at

167

women; it looks at women through feminist eyes and enables us to present our own vision of ourselves.

Along with the growth in numbers and in scholarship has come the emergence of Women's Studies programs and activities. We have discussed these programs in some detail in the first chapter. A brief review will help to illustrate the process of transformation to which these programs contribute. These programs and courses have usually begun by taking a multidisciplinary approach. Various established departments offer one or two courses in their particular discipline that focus on concerns relevant to women. Sometimes an interdisciplinary approach emerges. Instructors from two or more disciplines focus on the same problem or issue. Many Women's Studies programs combine a multidisciplinary approach and an interdisciplinary approach, leaving some courses in specific departments and offering interdisciplinary courses out of the Women's Studies program. Having at least some autonomy allows more space for creative and innovative courses and programs. Sometimes even a transdisciplinary approach emerges. Rather than approaching an issue by moving from discipline to discipline, a new vision is achieved that embodies and transcends several disciplines. Often these programs also manage to overcome the traditional "town and gown" dichotomy. Connections with the wider community develop. Sometimes the university program offers courses or programs that are open to the community. At other times community organizations or individuals help to organize or teach in the university program.

The vision that is emerging under the influence of these programs and courses has led to the recognition that the total academic curriculum is in need of change. Because the Academy has been established and developed by and for men, the curriculum is dominated by the male eye. Women's Studies programs have enabled us to open the other eye, but the newly opened eye has been isolated so that students and faculty move from seeing with one eye to seeing with the other. Seeing with both eyes open requires that the traditional curriculum be augmented and changed. Often the first attempt is an "add women and stir" approach. One unit of a course is devoted to women, or one day in each unit focuses on women. Textbooks add a section on women in relation to a topic. A reading or several readings by women are added to course requirements. Many institutions have adopted this sort of mainstreaming. A few schools have actually begun work on curriculum transformation. Institutes are held for retraining faculty to help them see how the vision of women can be fully integrated with the male vision (Howe 242). Courses are beginning to be developed that are truly coeducational. The visions and actions of men and women are presented in their interrelatedness as complementing and contributing to each other. Work is being done to provide suggestions and help for ways of curriculum transformation (Howe 270–84). Two particularly helpful works are *Toward a Balanced Curriculum: A Sourcebook for Initiating Gender Integration Projects,* by Bonnie Spanier, Alexander Bloom, and Darlene Boroviak, and *Women's Place in the Academy,* edited by Marilyn R. Schuster and Susan R. Van Dyne. These books contain discussions of issues that must be addressed by curriculum transformation: Who is missing from the curriculum? How can these people and groups be identified, recovered, and integrated into the educational process? They suggest ways in which institutions have and can develop programs of change; and they give helpful suggestions, including sample syllabi, for working on transformation in the classroom.

There is continued resistance to the development of women's vision. Some of this resistance remains at the level of admitting women into the Academy. Women still experience barriers in entering such fields as natural science, in obtaining jobs at prestigious institutions, and in securing tenured and higher-rank positions. Support for work in Women's Studies and for Women's Studies programs is often minimal. Budgets remain low and positions are staffed by part-time people or on a part-time basis. Faculty and administrators are forced to wear two or more hats and often are overworked in both positions. Other faculty are resistant to change, sometimes from lethargy and sometimes from sexism. The reward system in the Academy usually fails to recognize interdisciplinary work as significant, and so does not reward, or may even penalize, people for doing such work. Although society and the Academy are changing, prejudices are difficult to overcome, and backlash is a continual threat.

Yet the history of higher education in the United States gives some reason for hope. The old liberal arts curriculum of the classics and the Bible held sway from the seventeenth to the mid-nineteenth century. This curriculum was stable and required. The sciences made their way into this curriculum with difficulty at first and were added only at the fringes. Between 1870 and 1910, as more sciences were added, the curriculum began to be transformed. It was infused with a scientific ethos. The sciences moved from being electives to being required. Departments were firmly established and specialties emerged. Today this situation is defended as "traditional." Just as the nineteenth-century curriculum found that it could not simply "add science and stir," so also the late twentieth century may find that the presence of Women's Studies programs will work an equally extensive transformation of educational patterns (Howe 221–30).

The development and strengthening of this emerging vision lend support to the hope for transformation. Two important focuses are on language and method. These are issues that have been addressed many times in the essays in this book. They also emerge as central in efforts to transform the curriculum. All faculty members in all disciplines must use language. They read, write, lecture, direct seminars, and advise. Language is of central importance to the Academy, and so the focus on language is not surprising. Method is also fundamental to all of the Academy. In sketching the possibilities and promises that are emerging in the Academy because of feminist vision, these two focuses give us much valuable insight. They also reconfirm the process of change that we have seen emerge in the various disciplines, in Women's Studies, and in curriculum transformation.

The Transformation of Language

In the area of language and communication in the Academy, women have begun with the same approach that they have taken to specific disciplines. They have learned to use the "male" language. This has not been difficult to do in that women in English-speaking societies in general grow up learning an English that stresses the dominance and importance of the male and that trivializes or subordinates the female. Examples are abundant. Men are characterized by more positive adjectives: "strong," "dominant," "powerful," "active." Women are characterized as "weak," "subservient," "dependent," "passive." Male endings are used, and perpetuate exclusion of women from roles ("chairman"), and female endings, when used, tend to be diminutive ("poetess"). Masculine pronouns are used, and suppress the feminine. Using male language in the Academy usually only requires learning discipline-specific terminology, which is not difficult to accomplish. Women also grow up learning to move between women's forms of communication and men's forms of communication. They already know the basic rules of two related but different language games. As they move into the Academy, women simply use male structures of communication. Sometimes women academics remain at this stage of language usage and even make the claim that male structures and forms of communication are superior, although evidence would suggest that this strategy does not result in equal treatment (Frank and Anshen 49).

Often, however, women experience a lack or a problem with this language usage. This experience seems to have two sources. Again, as in the wider culture, women begin to experience the manner in which language excludes them. That all students and faculty are referred to by "he" and that all humans are spoken of as "men" is deeply disturbing. Women begin to recognize that these terms are really not gender-neutral. Acting as if these are gender-neutral words is the cause of much unfairness, confusion, and exclusion. When the masculine gender words are used they are understood to refer to men. It is difficult to image a woman in the role or position referred to by the masculine words. Elizabeth Dodson Gray's example of the child who cannot image herself as a doctor illustrates this problem. Mary Vetterling-Braggin has edited a volume, *Sexist Language,* that sets out many arguments related to these experiences. The discussions included in this book, as well as in others, such as Dennis Baron's *Grammar and Gender,* clearly show that language usage has contributed to the perpetuation of structures and practices of inequality. As Baron points out, implausible derivations have even been proposed in the attempt further to substantiate inequality by means of language. For example, he cites the folk etymology of "woman" set out by Robert Southey in 1847: "Look at the very name—Woman, evidently meaning either man's woe—or abbreviated from woe to man, because by woman was woe brought into the world" (34). Philosophical, sociological, and etymological studies all legitimate the suspicions about language that are raised by women's experiences.

Women may also experience another problem with language usage. Those who have women colleagues, especially feminist ones, may observe that communication with women takes on different forms than communication with men. Indeed, women may well experience exclusion in conversations with male colleagues. Men interrupt women, and studies carried out by Pamela Rishman indicate that "men get to talk more, at times of their own choosing, about topics which interest them" (Frank and Anshen 33). These studies suggest that for women to carry on conversations with men at a level that approaches equality, they must develop excellent verbal skills and must be constantly attentive not just to the topic of discussion, but also to the power dynamics at work within the conversation.

Studies indicate that women develop different styles of communication that are often used only with other women. Communication experiences that women have with other women give them a sense of a fuller range of human communication possibilities than are available in male styles only. An example of this experience of communication even offers a challenge to the metaphor that we have used to help give focus to this volume. Carol Gilligan's work in psychology has suggested that women speak "in a different voice." The recent study *Women's Ways of Knowing,* by Mary Field Belenky, Blythe McVicker Clinchy, Nancy Rule Goldberger, and Jill Mattuck Tarule, presses this claim farther. The authors suggest that women use metaphors of voice, of listening and silence, more than visual metaphors. They suggest that this indicates the importance of women's connectedness with, rather than separateness from, that which is to be understood (18). We will look further at their work later in this chapter. At this point in our discussion their work contributes to the insight that women's experiences with language suggest that language in the Academy is not fully human language.

One response to this recognition is to begin to ask for specific changes in language usage. Women and men in the Academy who have become aware of this problem have become sensitive to terminology and examples that they use. They have stopped using language and examples that demean and objectify women. They have begun using examples that show men, as well as women, in roles of parenting, and women, as well as men, in decision-making roles in the public sphere. To help with more inclusive language, usage guidelines have been formulated and used by publishers such as McGraw-Hill and Macmillan and by professional organizations such as the Association of American Colleges, the American Psychological Association, and the International Association of Business Communications. These guidelines suggest usages that do not exclude women and that make them more visible. They also suggest usages that do not stereotype men and thereby confine them to particular roles. Because of all this work and evidence, many campuses have concentrated on changing some specific language usages. Many campuses recognize the importance of having chairpersons and of printing materials that explain student opportunities by using both masculine and feminine gender pronouns.

Another response to the recognition of the power of language to perpetuate inequality has been to name things that have been ignored by not being spoken or have been inaccessible because they have not been named. In *Outrageous Acts and Everyday Rebellions* Gloria Steinem reviews some of the words that have emerged to name women's experiences. She says, "We have terms like *sexual harassment* and *battered* women. A few years ago, they were just called *life*" (149). We can now talk about such things as rape, sexual assault, lesbianism, reproductive freedom, pay equity, sexism, male chauvinism, and androgyny because we use the words and thereby name the experiences. Another important example of the activity of naming has been the development of the use of the title Ms., which enables women to identify themselves without doing so in terms of marital status.

Women have also begun to change language by reclaiming

173

words. Words that before had only negative connotations have begun to acquire positive connotations. Steinem notes: "The feminist spirit has reclaimed some words with defiance and humor. *Witch, bitch, dyke,* and other formerly pejorative epithets turned up in the brave names of small feminist groups" (154). Women in religion have begun to reclaim words like "goddess" and have begun to image God as mother. Perhaps the most important words to be reclaimed are "woman" and "women." To speak with pride of oneself as a woman is an important step in self-identity. But scholars have begun to show that we must also reclaim the plural, "women." If we ignore the differences in economic, political, racial, ethnic, and legal status among women, we continue to conceal who we are. The uncritical use of "woman" is apt to conceal the myth of the eternal feminine, the unchanging, nurturant, self-sacrificing wife and mother. Reclaiming the word women makes it clear that women are diverse and that their roles change over time and from culture to culture. This reclamation also helps to guard against the perception of women as passive victims of patriarchal oppression. In reclaiming the word, women begin to reclaim their strength.

Such language change is slow. As Audre Lorde says, "We must use the language of the patriarchs even as we think our way out of patriarchy" (233). Changing patriarchal language requires attentiveness and sensitivity. There is resistance to language change. People who benefit from the patriarchal structures are threatened by the critique of language. Moreover, as Mary Key notes in *Male/Female Language,* people in patriarchal structures are accustomed to change being initiated by men (133). They resist changes proposed by women.

Despite resistance, the focus on language has begun to move beyond the stage of language reform to that of transformation. The integration of women's vision into the Academy requires not only changes in specific language usage, but also consideration of the ways in which women find their voices. As already noted, studies are just beginning to emerge which indicate that many of the ways in which women communicate and articulate their knowledge are different from traditional male ways. This work is showing that women have developed ways of voicing themselves that are silenced, or even condemned, in the current

174

Academy. The implication for the Academy is that these ways of knowing need to be integrated into the Academy. This will require consideration of new ways of teaching and offers challenges and possibilities to the Academy for developing new and more humane ways of teaching and knowing. We will look at these issues in more detail after examining the transformation of method.

The Transformation of Method

A second focus of the developing feminist vision has been on method and objectivity. Again, the opening of the feminist eye begins a four-stage process that promises not just new possibilities for women, but more humane possibilities for all humans. As in all areas of the Academy, women began by learning the method of their disciplines. Although the various disciplines are at different stages in the development of methodological critique, there is a sense in which it is not inaccurate to say that scientific method is everywhere the same (Gadamer 9). In particular, method stresses the importance of scientific objectivity. Research is judged better when it is distanced from the object of research. Commitment to values is deemed destructive of the search for knowledge or truth.

As women have developed skills at using method that stresses objectivity, they have often begun to question this method, as Sandra Harding has done in *The Science Question in Feminism*. Out of reflection on their own experiences, women have begun to recognize that scientific method is not value-free or uncommitted. The feminist critique points to biases of sex, race, class, and imperialism in the eye of the beholder. Elizabeth Dodson Gray points out, that "reason is standpoint dependent." And Sandra Harding suggests that there is no such thing as "pure" science, untouched by social realities and values. The knower is always positioned somewhere in society and is either consciously or unconsciously influenced by that position. Bias can enter in the way we frame our questions to be investigated, for what is problematic for one group may be invisible to another. The factory owner supports research on time-and-motion studies to get more work for the same money. The workers struggle to raise questions about the effects of toxic chemicals in the workplace.

Bias enters again in the way we report and interpret observations. Male primatologists, seeing a single male ape in the midst of a group of females, report on a "harem," that is, a dominant male with first choice of food and sexual partners, leading and protecting a group of females. Jane Lancaster, surveying the same scene, writes:

> For a female, males are a resource in her environment which she can use to further the survival of herself and her offspring. If environmental conditions are such that the male role can be minimal, a one male group is likely. Only one male is necessary for a group of females if his only role is to impregnate them. (34)

Male biologists, studying the organization of the cell, developed a theory of "the master molecule," in which the DNA encodes and transmits all instructions for the unfolding of a living cell. Barbara McClintock's research on the genetics of corn

> yielded a view of DNA in delicate interaction with the cellular environment—an organismic view. . . . No longer is a master control to be found in a single component of the cell; rather control resides in the complex interactions of the entire system. (Keller 601)

The feminist vision is not alone in offering this critique of method. Much work has emerged from within the Academy that challenges scientific objectivity and method. Thomas Kuhn, in *The Structure of Scientific Revolutions,* develops an understanding of change in the natural sciences which argues that all scientific understanding is founded on a paradigm. Paradigms change when people begin to find anomalies. Science is not free of commitment, but is always situated in a context of commitment. Hans-Georg Gadamer has also offered, in *Truth and Method,* an important critique of method that emphasizes the inevitable role of prejudice or preunderstanding for all understanding. The social sciences have contributed to this critique by pointing to the realization that knowledge, even scientific knowledge, must be seen as socially constructed. Latour and

Wolgar's and Karin Knorr-Cetina's works have been of particular importance in this area. They observe scientists in the laboratory and identify how the modes of discourse and interpretive frameworks of these scientists contribute to what emerges as "fact."

Thus the feminist critique has joined many critiques of method and objectivity. All these critiques point to the need for the fourth stage of development. Concepts of method and of objectivity need to be transformed. All the contributors to this book, from Gray through Ruether, point to the need for methodological transformation. Sandra Harding shows most clearly that this transformation requires us to abandon claims to scientific objectivity that are based on the separation of the knower and the known. She writes:

> Objectivity never has been and could not be increased by value neutrality. Instead, it is commitment to anti-authoritarian, anti-elitist, participatory and emancipatory values and projects that increase the objectivity of science. (27)

The analysis of our commitments can lead to a transformation of method. As this transformation begins to occur, the possibilities and promises are great. If we can fully integrate the feminist vision, it is possible that a revolution akin to the Copernican revolution will emerge. We may find a way of envisioning ourselves that helps us to understand our fullest possibilities and so live more fully and freely.

Beginning a Transformation of Knowing

The hermeneutic of transformation that has developed within and been supported by feminist critique can be traced not only in the transformation of language and method, but also in the transformation of knowing. Women's experiences have critiqued and contributed to the understanding of how humans know. In the Academy this critique resulted in the movement to reevaluate traditional approaches to learning and teaching.

For understanding the transformation of knowing, which is only beginning to take place, it is important to recognize that the first stage of the process, gaining entry to the Academy, was part of a political movement. We have looked briefly at this political movement in chapter 1, but it is helpful to reiterate its importance here. It was the political movement that enabled women to raise their consciousnesses to an awareness of their own political position. It was also the political movement that gave women time and space in which to work out the implications of their experiences and insights and that enabled them to raise their aspirations individually and collectively. It takes time for pioneers, risking themselves in socially unacceptable roles, to enlarge the range of socially permissible behaviors and to gain numbers sufficient to begin to bring about change. Sally Gregory Kohlstedt illustrates the need for time in her article "In from the Periphery: American Women in Science, 1830–1880." She points out that it took three generations of women to open access for women to advanced scientific training and to membership in scientific societies. Women first worked as amateurs; then as popularizers, textbook writers, and illustrators; and then as organizers of special study groups and summer schools. Only then did they begin to enter the ranks of the professionals. In such work it takes support from an intimate circle if individuals are to avoid burnout or break down. The political movement of the late 1960s and the 1970s developed political structures known as consciousness-raising groups. These groups facilitated a change of consciousness for individual women, strengthened their self-esteem and self-confidence, and served as support and education structures as women moved into action.

The form of education that emerged within these groups was not traditional. Women shared experiences with one another and began to identify issues of concern, such as rape and health care. No one was an expert, and so all contributed to gathering and sharing knowledge. Collective structures that stressed equality and cooperation quickly emerged. In the collective that founded the Rape Crisis Centre in Toronto, for example, high school students, lawyers, Ph.D. candidates, and university faculty worked together and learned together without any emergence of hierarchical structures. Dale Spender writes:

> In attempting to describe feminist education, there is a limit to the use which can be made of the customary terms in education.

178

This was a learning experience, although qualitatively different
from the learning which many of us had "endured" in our own
schooling. It was part of living, not an activity which occurred
in prescribed places and at prescribed times. . . . The terms
"teacher" and "learner" . . . become meaningless in a feminist
context, where *all* are teaching and learning. (168)

New structures of education emerged in these groups outside
the Academy.

Charlotte Bunch and Sandra Pollack have edited a volume,
called *Learning Our Way*, that explains and characterizes some of
the feminist structures that have emerged as alternatives to
traditional structures of education. Nancy Schniedewind's article
in their volume summarizes some of the characteristics of feminist education and helps to depict the experience of education
that many women had before they entered work in the traditional Academy (261–71). Education could take place in an
atmosphere of "mutual respect, trust, and community" (262).
Feminist education stresses sharing rather than competition.
Knowledge and understanding are treated not as private com-
modities, but as being held in common. Moreover, leadership in
education can be shared. These structures outside the Academy
developed as collectives, as communities of colearners and
coteachers. This meant that hierarchy and disciplinary bound-
aries were not part of the structure. This cooperative education
was problem-centered, and so transdisciplinary. This approach
also resulted in these educational structures being action-ori-
ented. Education was carried out within the context of commitment to changes that would empower women. Finally, these
emerging structures stressed the need to integrate cognitive and
affective learning. Emotions, intuitions, relations, and insights
were integrated into the process of knowing rather than being
excluded.

Many women who entered the Academy in the 1970s
brought these experiences of feminist education with them. As
they moved into the "teacher" position in the Academy they
were aware that the model they were helping to perpetuate was
not the model that had empowered them. Paulo Freire, characterizing the traditional masculine model as "banking," writes:

The banking concept distinguishes two stages in the action of
the educator. During the first, he cognizes a cognizable object

while he prepares his lessons in his study or his laboratory; during the second, he expounds to his students about that object. The students are not called upon to know, but to memorize the contents narrated by the teacher. Nor do the students practice any act of cognition, since the object towards which that act should be directed is the property of the teacher. (67–68)

As women faculty began to recognize the ways in which this model incapacitates all students, especially women (Spender 170), they began to work for changes.

Some of these changes focused on classroom structures. Traditional classes were changed to allow for more expression of feeling and student exchange. Seating structures were changed to enable students to see one another, and faculty to move away from the lectern and into the class; subgroups were formed for discussion and for cooperative learning tasks. Students were given more opportunity to lead the class, and teachers learned how to give students more opportunity to explore ideas without faculty intervention. Grading practices were restructured to remove some of the impact of this relationship of power. Structures of learning other than the classroom situation were also developed. Students were encouraged to undertake independent work, field experiences, and cross-cultural experiences. Many of these changes were also effected by people who had experiences of political movements other than the feminist movement, such as the civil rights movement. The most significant change brought about by the feminist experience was, of course, the emergence of Women's Studies courses and programs. It was in this context that the feminist model of education, stressing interdisciplinary, cooperative, and committed learning, found room within the traditional Academy. Dale Spender describes the current situation as one in which the traditional patriarchal paradigm for education that does much to exclude women still dominates; however,

> along side this, often in the same institutions, and sometimes in the same departments, is a feminist model of education which not only challenges those boundaries, rules, definitions and methodologies, but which also posits female experience as a viable alternative for organizing the theory and practice of education. (171)

Women's Studies has provided the possiblity for the transformation of the Academy's understanding of the process of knowing and for the ways in which, as a result of this transformed understanding, it will go about its task of educating. Florence Howe suggests that this process of transformation should be seen as contributing to the goals of liberal education to be interdisciplinary and unifying, to develop critical skills of problem-solving, to develop capabilities of value judgment, and to promote socially useful ends (Boxer 681–82).

Transformation is just beginning, and it is difficult to envision all the possibilities that may emerge. A brief look at three recent works that contribute to this transformation will give some indication of emerging directions.

Theories of Women's Studies, edited by Gloria Bowles and Renate Duelli-Klein, examines the debate within Women's Studies as to whether it should maintain itself as an autonomous discipline or integrate into the other, longer-established disciplines. This question is vital to the process of transformation. If Women's Studies works for its own autonomy, the danger is that it will continue to exist as a marginal, underbudgeted part of the traditional institution. Its differences will be tolerated, but it will not be able to empower learners and transform the process of knowing. Those who argue for autonomy reflect on the importance that the political base has served for the process of the development of Women's Studies. If integration is chosen, the danger is that no transformation will occur. Traditional ways are powerful, and the likelihood is that they will prevail. Integration will not transform. Most of the contributors in *Theories of Women's Studies* suggest that both approaches must be taken and that they must be taken together. Moreover, many of the contributors emphasize the need for reflection on theory, on feminist methodology. Without such reflection, individual attempts at transformation may work against one another.

Two other recent works add insights to theoretical reflection and to visions of possible directions for transforming ways of knowing. The first is Carol Gilligan's influential book *In a Different Voice.* As Elizabeth Dodson Gray explains, Gilligan worked in psychology with Lawrence Kohlberg. Kohlberg's studies had set out a series of stages of moral decision-making.

Gilligan began with the intent of confirming his basic structure, which ranked highest those decision-makers who began with principles. Gilligan chose to study women who were deciding whether or not to have an abortion. What Gilligan discovered was that her subjects did not follow Kohlberg's pattern. As a result, Gilligan suggests that we need to take more seriously the type of moral reasoning that stresses relationship, connectedness, and care. Gilligan's contribution to the transformation of knowing is important because her work suggests that women may have developed ways of moral understanding that are important to a fuller understanding of human moral reasoning.

In like manner, *Women's Ways of Knowing,* by Belenky, Clinchy, Goldberger, and Tarule, suggests that at least five ways of knowing can be identified for women. These are silence, received knowledge, subjective knowledge, procedural knowledge, and constructed knowledge. These ways of knowing are put forward as a correction of William Perry's study of male college students. His study traces a student's epistemological development from a basic dualism to a final stage of commitment in relativity. Belenky and the other authors suggest that the 135 women in their study, women from diverse backgrounds, led them to find quite a different pattern in women's development. The five ways are not to be viewed as stages, for growth and movement may not always be through the series. Indeed, a person may use several of these ways at one time. In reading this volume most women in the Academy will probably be able to identify themselves as participating in all these ways of knowing.

The fifth way of knowing, constructed knowledge, is the most significant, for this way is not included in Perry's work and is virtually unrecognized in the Academy. The goals of constructed knowledge do not seem to be those of Perry's highest stage. The goals of this way of knowing are more ambiguous than Perry's commitment in relativity but are concerned with connection as a way of knowing. The implications of this examination for educating students are not yet fully worked out. The authors of *Women's Ways of Knowing* suggest that an important implication of their study is for the development of connected teaching where the teacher serves as midwife. They suggest that an adversarial, doubting style alienates women:

> Education conducted on the connected model would help women toward community, power, and integrity. Such an education could facilitate the development of women's minds and spirits rather than, as in so many cases reported in this book, retarding, arresting, or even reversing their growth. (228)

This work contains many promises and possibilities for ways of transforming the process of knowing in the Academy. If women come to know in these diverse ways, and if connected knowing has not been recognized by the Academy, then many new structures need to be developed to facilitate growth. Moreover, questions must be addressed as to what in the traditional model remains important to male and female development.

The project of developing a truly coeducational process of knowing presents the Academy with great challenges. In some ways the feminist critique threatens the Academy's traditional ways of learning and teaching. But at the same time the feminist experience of knowing offers the Academy rich possibilities for developing more fully human ways of learning and teaching.

Beyond the Academy

The possibilities for fuller human existence brought about by the integration of the female eye into human seeing are not restricted to the Academy. Indeed, the Academy often lags behind the wider society in terms of its acceptance of diverse and new visions. Many women have left the Academy in order to pursue life-styles that more fully actualize the possibilities and promises of their emerging insights. Other women have not been concerned with the transformation of the Academy, but have worked in other areas of society. Some of the areas are like the Academy in that women have first had to gain entrance before the process of transformation can begin. In many areas of life, women are already present and recognized as important participants. In these areas the movement toward transformation shows clear promise and suggests many possibilities. A recent work that does an excellent job of characterizing the wide range of transformations taking place in the total culture is Elinor Lenz and Barbara Meyerhoff's *The Feminization of America*. This work looks at the manner in which women's values are changing public and private life in America. The authors cover such areas as friendship, work, family, health care, art, peace, and spirituality. We will not here attempt to deal with all these transformations. Yet, because the transformation in the Academy has been so dependent on political structures and support structures outside the Academy, it seems important to conclude this examination by returning to a recognition of the transformation in the broader society. We will look briefly at how feminist work is transforming the human relation to nature and to other humans. Then we will conclude with an examination of how feminism is transforming spiritual life.

Nature and human relations. All of us in our daily lives stand in relation to nature. We eat and breathe, seek shelter, grow, change, seek health, and die. Many of the activities we are engaged in because we share in the natural order have traditionally been included in the sphere of women's work. But the manner in which humans have conceptualized their relation to nature has been hierarchical. People see themselves as "masters" of nature, and control nature at will. As women more fully introduce their experiences into this vision it is possible that all humans will begin to see themselves as part of nature rather than above it. Our images of ourselves as having dominion may change to an image of nurturing, or even interdependence. Women's involvement in peace movements exemplifies such possibilities. Faced with the reality of nuclear weapons, women tend to reject concepts of "limited nuclear war." Women's experience of closeness to nature informs this judgment.

Growing feminist insights also show possibilities for transforming human relationships. If we can see that our differences are not primarily ways of ranking and dominating, but provide us with ways of naturally enriching one another's lives, fuller human relations can emerge. Again, women have experience that has stressed nurturing and mediation. As these skills are more consciously valued, it is possible for us to develop more accepting human relations. Some changes in family structures exemplify the promise of these developing relationships. In many families, parenting has become an activity that women and men share. Often when parents share in caring for and nurturing their children, they also begin to transform their relations with their children from authority relations to cooperative ones. We have also become more able to recognize "nontraditional" family structures as nurturing and healthy, rather than as inadequate because of the lack of a hierarchical and paternalistic structure.

The example of health illustrates the way in which feminist understanding is helping to bring about transformation of human relations to nature and other humans. Women have long been part of health care. Although once they were primarily responsible for health care, in the contemporary system women have been patients or secondary care-takers, nurses. Women's experiences with the contemporary health care system have been characterized by lack of control. This is perhaps best illustrated by physicians taking over childbirth. Many of our grandmothers delivered their children with the help of a local midwife, family member, or family physician. But many of our mothers were anesthetized and would say that the doctor, usually male, delivered their children. Winning back control over our bodies thus became an early and important focus of the current feminist movement. Barbara Ehrenreich and Deirdre English write, in *Complaints and Disorders: The Sexual Politics of Sickness:*

> Medical science has been one of the most powerful sources of sexist ideology in our culture. Justifications for sexual discrimination . . . must ultimately rest on the one thing that differentiates women from men; their bodies. Theories of male superiority ultimately rest on biology. Medicine stands between biology and social policy . . . biology traces the origins of disease; doctors pass judgment on who is sick and who is well. *Medicine's prime contribution to sexist ideology has been to describe women as sick, and as potentially sickening to men.* (5; italics added)

In response to this situation the feminist movement has developed ways of enabling women to understand and claim their bodies.

185

The feminist movement has worked for change in health care in a number of ways: helping women redefine themselves as healthy, providing information and education, identifying and addressing sexist beliefs, and working for control of reproduction (Elston 202). Women have found many ways to work on these issues. The Boston Women's Health Collective's *Our Bodies, Ourselves* (in the new edition *The New Our Bodies, Ourselves*) has been the definitive work for women to use to educate themselves about their own bodies. This work, probably more than any other, has enabled women to reach one of the goals of the collective: to take "greater charge of their own health care and their lives" (xiii).

Women's groups such as the Boston Collective have established clinics where women can learn about their bodies and obtain professional care that is not sexist. For example, victims of rape have been able to go to these clinics and obtain medical care without being subjected to the traumatic ordeal of the type of medical examination that may well be experienced as a second rape. Women find that medical professionals who choose to work in such clinics accept women's experiences of their own bodies as legitimate and informed.

Women's work to control their own bodies has also changed what is considered acceptable birthing procedure. Although most births still take place in hospitals, and although there is still much intervention in childbirth, many of us have been able to deliver our children without intervention. Hospitals allow fathers, but not others, in the delivery area; some hospitals provide birthing rooms. Midwives still find practice difficult. The health care industry, which makes money on childbirth, works against the advance of midwifery and alternative birthing, such as home delivery (Lenz and Meyerhoff 128). However, in many places these options are available.

A final example of the changes in health care that have emerged with the help of the feminist movement is holistic medicine. As in other areas in which feminism has had an impact, the impetus has been toward overcoming dichotomies and toward empowerment. Holistic medicine stresses the importance of treating the whole person. Lenz and Meyerhoff identify some characteristics of holistic medicine:

- being concerned with healing the split between mind and body;
- focusing on each individual's biological and cultural uniqueness and custom-tailoring treatments to individual needs;
- viewing health as a positive state rather than as an absence of illness;
- encouraging the individual's responsibility and capacity for self-care and self-healing; and
- emphasizing nutrition and exercise in promoting and maintaining health (125–26).

All these goals are supported by and reinforce feminist work.

Much remains to be done in transforming health care. Medical school textbooks still lack understanding of female sexuality (Elston 200) and frequently make use of sexist rhetoric. The nursing profession continues, with mixed success, to work for more decision-making power and recognition. Medical costs and government cuts in funding continue to exclude many people from health care. This is especially disastrous for poor, pregnant women. But the transformations that have occurred should not be underestimated.

Women have begun to claim control over their bodies in ways that emphasize the experience of a connectedness with nature. As Elizabeth Dodson Gray explains so well, these insights into our connectedness may be what enable humans to live more appropriately with nature and with one another. When we understand and embrace our natural existence we begin to relate more easily and humanly to others, female and male.

Religious life. The women's movement has had a significant impact on religious life in all groups in the United States: Catholic, Protestant, and Jewish; black, white, and Hispanic; left wing and right wing. In fact, the antifeminist backlash from the religious right is a testimony to the depth of the vision and the extent of the activities among those who define themselves as religious feminists. "The mistake," one observer wryly remarked, about the American nuns in conflict with the Vatican "was in teaching them to read."

Certainly as awareness of the sexism and misogyny of existing religious traditions has grown, increasing numbers of women (and some men) have sought spiritual nourishment in alternative groupings, including Catholic nongeographic parishes, Jewish havuroth, Protestant "house churches," feminist liturgical groups, and Wicca covens. Some groups are informal, having ten or twelve friends meeting in one another's homes. Others are highly organized, with educational and political agendas. These include The Women's Ordination Conference, WATER (Women's Alliance for Theology, Ethics and Ritual), Black Women in Church and Society, Women's Theological Center, and Women-Church Convergence. The latter group, a successor to the Catholic Women of the Church Coalition, sees itself as facilitating the growth of a wider ecumenical women-church movement, that is, the community of believers, men as well as women, who are struggling to free themselves and their institutions from patriarchy. These groups (no one knows how many there are) have in common the attempt to find new inclusive language, new imagery and symbols, and new forms of worship that both express and expand the new understanding of ourselves and our relationships to one another and to the transcendent.

The vision is being articulated chiefly by writers on feminist theologies and spiritualities. It is noteworthy that there are more theologically trained women in the world today than ever before in human history. As Rosemary Radford Ruether remarks,

> the present decade is the first time in known history in which large numbers of women have been able to gain both the educational means and the collective strength to challenge the redemptive meaning of biblical religion for women and either demand significant transformation of its traditional understandings or else call for a rejection of biblical religion altogether in favor of an alternative women's religion. (Ruether, *Beyond Domination* 108)

These women pose the question bluntly: Is Christianity irredeemably sexist? The countercultural feminists answer with a resounding yes, and turn to the ancient nature religions, to the mother goddesses of the Mediterranean world, or to contemporary feminist Wicca with its poetic nature rituals. But other religious feminists, among them Gray, Ruether, and Fiorenza, find prophetic elements in the biblical tradition that they use both in an unsparing critique of the sexism and misogyny of the dominant patriarchal traditions and as a basis for a radical reconstruction of the religious vision.

It is always difficult to put forth an alternative vision: our imaginations are limited by our historical circumstances, our very language is against us, calling up old meanings and associations. Nevertheless, liberationist feminists are seeing beyond gender, recasting the old polarities of spirit/matter, god/world, mind/body, self/other, transcendent/immanent, male/female in a new way. They move from a static to a process orientation, a vision of the universe as evolving. As a metaphor for creation they reject the image of the potter and the pot and with it the notion of a creator who is immutable pure spirit, external to creation and exercising absolute dominion over it. They turn for insight instead to a metaphor of birthing, envisioning a world evolving within a matrix or ground of being (Ruether, *Women and Men* 412). They speak of a divine energy progressively revealed in an evolving universe in which spirit and matter are the inside and the outside of the same process. They question the model of hierarchy that starts with God as pure spirit and moves down the chain of being to nonspiritual matter as the most inferior and dominated point in the chain of command, a model that symbolizes woman as more material and bodily than man (Ruether, *Sexism and God-Talk* 85–86).

In this evolving universe human consciousness is not seen as a spirit unfortunately imprisoned in a physical body. Rather,

> consciousness comes to be seen as the most intense and complex form of the inwardness of material energy itself as it bursts forth at the evolutionary level where matter is organized in the most complex and intensive way—the central nervous system and the cerebral cortex of the human brain. (Ruether, *Sexism and God-Talk* 86)

Human beings are thus placed within nature, not outside or above it. Gray's metaphor of humankind as a fetus in the womb of the world exemplifies this. Humans are part of a complex ecosystem, on which they depend, but this ecosystem does not derive from or depend on them.

If we understand human consciousness as the interiority of our bodies, then salvation or liberation does not consist in chastising the body to bring it into subjection (1 Corinthians 9:27), or in hoping for an eventual flight from the body into a realm of pure spirit. Rather, human development depends on centering down, overcoming alienation from our bodies and our repressed capacities, and building an authentic identity based on self-acceptance (Ruether, *Sexism and God-Talk* 264). Moreover, human autonomy and God's will are no longer cast in total opposition to each other, an opposition that can only be resolved by total self-abnegation and blind obedience (Ruether, *Women and Men* 413). Rather, the encounter with the divine is experienced as the discovery of the empowering spirit who founds our self-actualization (Ruether, *Sexism and God-Talk* 69).

The critique of domination/submission as a model for divine/human relations implies a similar critique for the relations of self to others. Not domination, but mutuality, interaction, participation become the keynotes for relationships in the family, the workplace, the government, and the community of nations.

Finally, immanence and transcendence take on new meanings. Transcendence is no longer seen as a flight from this world with its coming-to-be and passing-away, but as a breaking out of false consciousness into authenticity and the healing of broken relationships with our bodies, other people, and nature (Ruether, *Sexism and God-Talk* 71). Immanence is not conceived as static, stifling submergence in matter. Rather, "the God of Exodus who is the foundation . . . of our being and our new being embraces both the roots of our existence (matter) and also the endlessly new creative potential (spirit)" (Ruether, *Sexism and God-Talk* 70).

We need new language to name this reality. The Latin *dominus* was used to name God, Christ, the bishop, the feudal lord, the husband. Feminist critique has made clear how this naming reinforces the structures of domination and submission. To name God "mother" or "queen" may have some value in awakening us to the patriarchal character of our language, but it still carries too many old connotations. Ruether suggests:

> Our images of God as mother, father or parent mislead because of the distorted way these roles have been structured in human

relations, which any such language then functions to sanction and perpetuate, rather than to transform in redeeming directions. Perhaps what we need is not a further abstraction, but greater enrichment of our roots in divine life in the language of taste and touch and smell: God as Bread, Water, breath of life and odor of sanctity; above all, God as Friend, who does not alienate us from but connects us with our truest selves. (*Women and Men* 415)

The Hope in the Emerging Vision

Within the Academy and outside the Academy the emerging vision that enables us to see with both eyes open is offering promise and possibilities. Certainly there is resistance to these new possibilities. We are a technological culture and are open to change brought to us by technology. We want new gadgets, computers, videocassette recorders. We are willing to accept new ways of doing things, from child-rearing to cosmetic production and use of nuclear power, if they can be shown to be technical advances. But our technology embodies and reaffirms a model of domination and control. As Harding writes;

> mind versus nature and body, reason versus emotion and social commitment, subject versus object and objectivity versus subjectivity, the abstract and general versus the concrete and particular—in each case we are told that the former must dominate the latter lest human life be overwhelmed by irrational and alien forces symbolized in science as the feminine. (125)

It is difficult to change a culture's vision when it is so totally committed to scientific objectivity and when change is being suggested from the viewpoint that has been most devalued.

Yet, as the feminist eye remains open, there is hope that deeper perception will continue to develop. Feminism insists on the validity of the subjective, on the need to unite cognitive and affective; it emphasizes holism, cooperation, and complexity. Incorporation of these into a fuller vision of reality may be what our technological age needs to help us prevent the annihilation of humankind and much of the rest of the natural order.

Works Cited

Baron, Dennis, *Grammar and Gender.* New Haven, CT: Yale University Press, 1986.

Belenky, Mary Field, Blythe McVicker Clinchy, Nancy Rule Goldberger, and Jill Mattuck Tarule. *Women's Ways of Knowing.* New York: Basic Books, 1986.

Boston Women's Health Collective. *The New Our Bodies, Ourselves.* New York: Simon & Schuster, 1985.

Bowles, Gloria, and Renate Duelli-Klein, eds. *Theories of Women's Studies.* Boston: Routledge & Kegan Paul, 1983.

Boxer, Marilyn J. "For and About Women: The Theory and Practice of Women's Studies in the United States." *Signs* 7 (1982):661–95.

Bunch, Charlotte, and Sandra Pollack, eds. *Learning Our Way, Essays in Feminist Education.* Trumansburg, NY: The Crossing Press, 1983.

Ehrenreich, Barbara, and Deirdre English. *Complaints and Disorders: The Sexual Politics of Sickness.* Old Westbury, NY: Feminist Press, 1973.

Elston, Mary Ann. "Medicine as 'Old Husbands' Tales': The Impact of Feminism." In *Men's Studies Modified,* edited by Dale Spender. Elmsford, NY: Pergamon Press, 1981.

Fiorenza, Elisabeth Schüssler. *In Memory of Her: A Feminist Theological Reconstruction of Christian Origins.* New York: Crossroad, 1983.

Frank, Francine, and Frank Anshen. *Language and the Sexes.* Albany: State University of New York Press, 1983.

Freire, Paulo. *Pedagogy of the Oppressed.* New York: Seaview, 1971.

Gadamer, Hans-Georg. *Truth and Method.* New York: Seabury Press, 1975.

Gilligan, Carol. *In a Different Voice.* Cambridge, MA: Harvard University Press, 1982.

Graham, Patricia Alberg. "Expansion and Exclusion: A History of Women in American Higher Education." *Signs* 3 (1978):759–73.

Harding, Sandra. *The Science Question in Feminism.* Ithaca, NY: Cornell University Press, 1986.

Howe, Florence. *Myths of Coeducation.* Bloomington: Indiana University Press, 1984.

Keller, Evelyn Fox. "Feminism and Science." *Signs* 7 (1982):589–602.

Key, Mary. *Male/Female Language.* Metuchen, NJ: Scarecrow Press, 1975.

Knorr-Cetina, Karin. *The Manufacture of Knowledge.* Oxford: Pergamon Press, 1981.

Kohlstedt, Sally Gregory. "In from the Periphery: American Women in Science, 1830–1880." *Signs* 4 (1978):81–96.

Kuhn, Thomas. *The Structure of Scientific Revolutions,* 2d ed. Chicago: University of Chicago Press, 1970.

Lancaster, J. B. *Primate Behavior and the Emergence of Human Culture.* New York: Holt, Rinehart & Winston, 1975.

Latour, Bruno, and Steve Wolgar. *Laboratory Life: The Social Construction of Scientific Facts.* Beverly Hills, CA: Sage, 1979.

Lenz, Elinor, and Barbara Meyerhoff. *The Feminization of America.* Los Angeles: Jeremy P. Tarcher, 1985.

Lerner, Gerda. *The Creation of Patriarchy.* New York: Oxford University Press, 1986.

Lorde, Audre. "The Master's Tool Will Never Dismantle the Master's House." In *This Bridge Called My Back,* edited by Cherrie Moraga and Gloria Anzaldua. Watertown, MA: Persephone Press, 1981.

Owens, Jerry Sue. "Survival Skills for Educational Leaders in Higher Education," Women in Higher Education Conference. Orlando, FL, January 23, 1987.

Perry, William. *Forms of Intellectual and Ethical Development in the College Years.* New York: Holt, Rinehart & Winston, 1970.

Ricoeur, Paul. *Freud and Philosophy: An Essay on Interpretation.* New Haven, CT: Yale University Press, 1970.

Ruether, Rosemary Radford. *Sexism and God-Talk.* Boston: Beacon Press, 1983.

———. "Sexism, Religion, and the Social and Spiritual Liberation of Women Today." In *Beyond Domination,* edited by Carol C. Gould. Totowa, NJ: Rowman & Allanheld, 1983.

———. "Sexism and God-Talk." In *Women and Men, the Consequences of Power,* edited by Dana V. Hiller and Robin Ann Sheets. Cincinnati: Office of Women's Studies, University of Cincinnati, 1977.

Schuster, Marilyn R., and Susan R. Van Dyne, eds. *Woman's Place in the Academy.* Totowa, NJ: Rowman & Allanheld, 1985.

Segundo, Juan Luis. *The Liberation of Theology.* Maryknoll, NY: Orbis Books, 1976.

Spanier, Bonnie, Alexander Bloom, and Darlene Boroviak, eds. *Toward a Balanced Curriculum: A Sourcebook for Initiating Gender Integration Projects.* Cambridge, MA: Schenkman, 1984.

Spender, Dale, ed. *Men's Studies Modified.* Elmsford, NY: Pergamon Press, 1981.

Steinem, Gloria. *Outrageous Acts and Everyday Rebellions.* New York: Henry Holt, 1983.

Vetterling-Braggin, Mary, ed. *Sexist Language.* Totowa, NJ: Littlefield, Adams, 1981.

Index

Fiorenza, Elisabeth Schüssler 166, 188
First International Festival of Women's Film 101
Fischl, Eric 92
Fish, Janet 80–82
Flack, Audrey 89, 92
Fragonard, Jean 75
Frankenthaler, Helen 90
Franklin, Rosalin 10
Free market 111–12, 115, 120–24, 128–29
Freire, Paulo 179
Freud 62, 64
Friedan, Betty 11
Friedman, Milton, and Rose 112, 114, 120–21, 124, 129
Fuller, Margaret 17–18

Gadamer, Hans-Georg 176
Galileo 41
Garcia, Anna Maria 106
Garfinkel, Irwin 118, 125
Garrett, Mary Elizabeth 141
Gender xvi, 2, 27, 32, 67, 111–13, 118, 130, 134, 137–39, 149, 165, 171, 173, 189
Genesis 35, 38, 42–43, 45
Gentileschi, Artemisia 82, 84–85, 88
Gilder, George 112, 115–19, 124–26, 129
Gilligan, Carol 31, 69, 172, 181
Gilman, Charlotte Perkins 14
Giovanni, Nikki 15
God xvii, 35, 38–39, 43–46, 48, 53–55, 149, 153, 155–58, 160–61, 174, 190–91
God language 155–56
Goddess 174
Godmilow, Jill 103, 105, 108
Goldberger, Nancy Rule 172
Goldfarb, Lyn 105
Grandmother Movies 104
Grant, Joanne 105–6
Graves, Nancy 90

Gray, Elizabeth Dodson xv, 1, 171, 175, 177, 187–88
Gray, Lorraine 105, 109
Green Paradise Lost 32
Grimké, Angelina, and Sara 159

Haines, Randa 107
Hals, Frans 10
Hamilton, Alexander 58–59
Hammond, Harmony 90
Harding, Sandra xvii, 175, 177, 191
Haveman, Robert 118, 125
Health care 19, 185–87
Heckerling, Amy 107
Heller, Rita 109
Hepworth, Barbara 90
Hermeneutic 165–66, 177
Hesse, Eva 90
Heyward, Carter 54
Hierarchical 35, 48, 55, 63, 178
Hierarchy xv, 31, 39, 48, 100, 153, 157, 159, 189
History xv–xvi, 1–2, 13–14, 17–18, 25, 27–28, 47, 51, 58–69, 70–72, 75, 85, 89–90, 96–98, 105, 126, 128, 136, 139–40, 157, 161, 163, 165, 169, 188
Hollywood 97–98, 102–3, 106–8
Howard, Linda 72
Howe, Florence 9, 12, 19
Humanities xviii, 16
Hunter, Alberta 16
Hurston, Zora Neale 14
Hutchinson, Ann 14

Interdisciplinary xv, 13–14, 168–69, 180–81
Interpretation xvi, 3, 27, 74, 77, 85, 111, 134, 137–38, 160–61, 163, 166

Janson, H. W. 90
Jefferson, Thomas 58–59
Jencks, Christopher 119

Mott, Lucretia 14, 159
Mudd, Victoria 109
Mulvey, Laura 103
Muñoz, Susana 109
Murray, Elizabeth 90

Napier, B. Davie 42
National Organization of Women
    (NOW) 8, 11
National Women's Studies
    Association (NWSA) 12, 20
Natural science 16, 169, 176
Neel, Alice 72–80
Network television 98, 103, 108
Nevelson, Louise 72, 90
Noschese, Christine 109
Novak, Michael 123

Objectivity xvii, 128, 138, 175–
    77, 191
O'Keefe, Georgia 90
Our Bodies, Ourselves 186
Oxenberg, Jan 99

Painter 71–73, 75, 77, 80–83, 85,
    88–90, 92
Parkinson, Michelle 107, 109
Patriarchy xvii, 2, 28, 32, 39, 148–
    63, 174, 189
Patriarchy as a Conceptual Trap 30
Paul 31, 155
Peace 11, 162, 184
Pearlstein, Philip 74, 80
Pepper, Beverly 72, 90
Perry, William 182
Pfaff, Judy 90
Phenix, Lucy Massie 109
Phillips, J. B. 45
Philosophy xv, 31, 64, 100, 124,
    139, 149
Piscopia, Elena Lucrezia
    Cornaro 70
Piven, Frances 114, 124
Plath, Sylvia 66
Political 4, 7, 15, 17, 19, 60–61,

71, 93, 106, 124, 129, 131,
    135, 140, 150–51, 159–60,
    174, 178, 183, 188
Pollack, Sandra 179
Pomodoro, Arnaldo 90
Porete, Marguerite 153
Portillo, Lourdes 107, 109
Portraiture xvi, 72–80, 88
Potter, David 60
Priestley, Joanna 109
Profession(s) 4–6, 18–19, 71, 152,
    160, 187
Professional 9, 11, 16, 70–72, 112,
    151–52, 173, 178, 186

Quaker 59, 68, 160

Racism 21, 28, 106, 117, 136
Rainer, Yvonne 103
Rankin, Jeanette 4
Rape 11, 15, 44, 85, 104, 151,
    173, 178, 186
Reagan administration 111–12,
    115, 123
Rehnquist, William 162
Reichert, Julia xvi, 16
Reiter, Rayna 15
Religion xvii, 11, 17, 44, 151,
    163, 174, 187–91
Research xvii, 7, 9, 11, 13–14, 24,
    62, 68, 93, 113, 115, 118–19,
    129–30, 136–37, 139, 141–42,
    175–76
Rich, Adrienne 66
Richards, Ellen Swallow 7–8
Ricoeur, Paul 166
Riesman, David 20
Rishman, Pamela 172
Rosenberg, Jan 101
Rosenfelt, Deborah S. 13
Ross, Heather 116
Rothenberg, Susan 90
Rothschild, Amalie 101, 105
Rousseau, Jean 64